THE

REAL ESTATE INVESTING
Answer Book

THE

REAL ESTATE INVESTING
Answer Book

DENISE L. EVANS

ATTORNEY AT LAW

SPHINX® PUBLISHING
AN IMPRINT OF SOURCEBOOKS, INC.®
NAPERVILLE, ILLINOIS
www.SphinxLegal.com

First Edition, 2008

Published by: **Sphinx® Publishing, An Imprint of Sourcebooks, Inc.®**

<u>Naperville Office</u>
P.O. Box 4410
Naperville, Illinois 60567-4410
630-961-3900
Fax: 630-961-2168
www.sourcebooks.com
www.SphinxLegal.com

This publication is designed to provide accurate and authoritative information in regard to the subject matter covered. It is sold with the understanding that the publisher is not engaged in rendering legal, accounting, or other professional service. If legal advice or other expert assistance is required, the services of a competent professional person should be sought.

From a Declaration of Principles Jointly Adopted by a Committee of the American Bar Association and a Committee of Publishers and Associations

This product is not a substitute for legal advice.

Disclaimer required by Texas statutes.

Library of Congress Cataloging-in-Publication Data

Evans, Denise L.

The real estate investing answer book : your 300 top real estate money-making questions answered / by Denise Evans. -- 1st ed.

p. cm.

Includes index.

ISBN 978-1-57248-647-8 (pbk. : alk. paper) 1. Real estate investment--United States. 2. Real estate investment. I. Title.

HD255.E953 2007

332.63'240973--dc22

2007043269

Printed and bound in the United States of America.

VP — 10 9 8 7 6 5 4 3 2 1

Contents

Chapter 1

ROADBLOCKS— WHAT'S KEEPING YOU FROM INVESTING?

- I have no cash savings. Do I need a down payment in order to invest in real estate?
- Will bad credit keep me back?
- If my credit score needs improvement, how soon should I start working on improving it?
- My credit score is not going to get any better for a while. Can I still invest?
- If a bank will not finance me, why would a seller?
- My credit situation has me distressed enough. Why should I buy distressed properties?
- If someone else cosigns a note with me, won't my poor credit score pull his or her credit score down, too?
- None of my friends or relatives will cosign a note with me, I have no ability to borrow money without a cosigner, and I have very little cash. Can I still invest?
- I have cash and other assets, but I have a bad credit score for reasons beyond my control. Why would a lender focus on the one bad item and ignore everything else?
- I have a large mortgage on my home, car notes, and student loans. I will not qualify for additional debt. How can I invest in real estate?
- What if I make a bad decision?
- How do I find out more about investing in real estate?
- What do I do next?

Often, goals seem to be unreachable because of all the roadblocks in our way. The trick is to not let yourself become discouraged and overwhelmed. Look at one roadblock at a time, and then ask yourself the following questions.

- Is the roadblock real or just a myth?
- Is there a way to fix the roadblock?
- Is there a way around the roadblock?
- Is there a way to manage the roadblock?
- Is there a way to make the roadblock disappear forever?

Once you read through the following questions, you will be surprised to find that the roadblocks in your way can all be overcome, and nothing will be left standing in the way of you and your dreams of investing in real estate.

I have no cash savings. Do I need a down payment in order to invest in real estate?

You do not always need a down payment in order to invest in real estate. Although most lenders will require a 20–25% down payment, there are circumstances that will allow you to obtain 100% financing. These include:

- seller financing;
- property in need of repairs; and,
- purchasing a home in which you will live for some period of time.

Consumers, even those with relatively poor credit, can often borrow the full purchase price of a home they plan to occupy, *plus* enough extra money to cover closing costs. The interest rates are usually about the same as commercial loans for investment property.

Typically, people can borrow money fairly cheaply in order to buy a home if they have good credit and at least a 20% down payment. Loans for investment or business properties are usually at somewhat higher interest rates. On the other hand, if you do not have any down payment money, you will pay a higher interest rate than other homeowners, but about the same interest rate as or only slightly more than other investors.

With a no-money-down loan, you will typically have to live in the home for some period of time, generally two years. That might seem like a long time, but you will spend that long looking for a better deal. At the end of two years, you can rent the house out and look for another one to buy for your new residence. You may need to refinance your former home or renegotiate the terms with the lender so you can obtain the consumer interest rates and terms on your new dwelling. If you continue doing this every two years, you will soon have a very impressive investment portfolio.

Will bad credit keep me back?

"Bad" credit is not always as bad as you think, and even bad credit will not always prevent you from investing.

Lenders cannot make money unless they make loans. Not very many people have perfect credit scores. If people with perfect credit scores were the only ones able to borrow money, then most of the mortgage companies in the United States would be out of business.

You should learn your credit score, interview different lenders to see what their requirements are, and work on ways to improve your score if necessary. You can find more information on credit scores in Chapter 21.

If my credit score needs improvement, how soon should I start working on improving it?

You should start working on your credit score immediately.

It usually takes six months to one year of good credit practices to significantly increase your score. You will need to obtain all three credit reports, correct all mistakes, delete any old information that is no longer allowed on your report under federal law, and then focus on bringing up your score. You can do it, but it takes time. Be sure to read Chapter 21 on credit scores.

My credit score is not going to get any better for a while. Can I still invest?

There are opportunities for you to buy property, even with a terrible credit score that prevents any traditional lender financing. They include:

- seller financing;
- buying tax-sale, foreclosure-sale, or demolition-ordered properties;
- obtaining a cosigner or guarantor for the note;
- buying options; and,
- a large cash-down payment.

These topics are covered in more detail later.

If a bank will not finance me, why would a seller?

Most sellers do not do credit checks, especially if you have a 10–20% down payment. Sometimes a seller will finance you with no down payment at all. See Chapter 23 on seller financing for more information.

This alternative is much more common than you might think, for a variety of reasons. Some sellers need to reinvest their sale proceeds in something else. They can earn (1) relatively low interest rates from a financial institution; (2) higher returns from somewhat risky stocks and bonds with unpredictable earnings; or, (3) dependable mortgage payments from a property they know will hold its value. The third choice is often the most attractive.

Other sellers have properties that are overpriced for the marketplace. They might be willing to hold the financing to compensate for the higher price you are willing to pay.

My credit situation has me distressed enough. Why should I buy distressed properties?

A distressed property is one that has very large real or imagined problems—a looming foreclosure, a local government demolition threat for safety reasons, or a hazardous waste issue. These can be good purchases for any investor, but they are particularly valuable if you cannot borrow money. Read Chapters 4 and 5 for more details.

If someone else cosigns a note with me, won't my poor credit score pull his or her credit score down, too?

Borrowers' credit scores are not linked to each other. Even husbands and wives each have their own scores. A cosigner can be affected if you *default* on the loan he or she signed with you, or if you pay late, but not simply because he or she cosigned your loan.

A *cosigner* is a person who signs on the loan with the original borrower. The payment history for the loan will be shared with the credit reporting agencies for all parties as each payment is made. A *guarantor*, on the other hand, is someone who signs a separate agreement saying that he or she will pay if you default on your obligations. There is no credit reporting for the guarantor unless the borrower defaults and the guarantor then does not pay.

None of my friends or relatives will cosign a note with me, I have no ability to borrow money without a cosigner, and I have very little cash. Can I still invest?

As has already been briefly discussed, seller financing is a possibility. Options are another way to invest in real estate without having to borrow any money. It is a type of property flipping, but much less risky. Chapter 7 has more detailed information on options. You will need some cash, but it can be much less than you might otherwise require for a down payment.

> **Example:** Donald knows that Jane is willing to sell her property. He also knows she does not want to have signs on her land and does not want to deal with real estate agents. Jane wants $120,000 for her property, but Donald knows that similar properties routinely sell for $150,000. Donald can tell Jane: "I will pay you $1,000 if you will give me the right to buy your property any time in the next ninety days for $120,000. Whether I decide to purchase your house or not, you keep the $1,000. If I buy the property, the $1,000 is not credited against the purchase price, because it is payment for the contract you and I are making today. If I do not buy, you keep the $1,000."
>
> If Jane agrees to this option contract, Donald can find another buyer at the $150,000 price and make a quick $29,000 profit ($30,000 minus the $1,000 he spent to buy the option.) This is a very good investment opportunity for many people.

I have cash and other assets, but I have a bad credit score for reasons beyond my control. Why would a lender focus on the one bad item and ignore everything else?

Lenders would not do this. Cash talks. Just because you have a bad credit score does not mean you are without resources. Lenders are always willing to overlook a bad credit score if you have a large down payment because they know (1) you are much less likely to allow foreclosure if you have substantial equity; and, (2) even if they do have to foreclose, they can almost certainly resell the property for at least the amount of their loan.

Ironically, it is easier for someone with a poor credit score to invest in real estate than it is for him or her to buy a home. Commercial lending officers generally have more discretion than home mortgage lenders. If you have a good explanation regarding why a temporary situation seriously depressed your credit score, and you have a large down payment or other sizeable assets to pledge, you can invest and receive competitive interest rates.

I have a large mortgage on my home, car notes, and student loans. I will not qualify for additional debt. How can I invest in real estate?

Consumer lending is based on your personal income and the size of your other debts. A real estate investment stands on its own feet. If the anticipated income from the specific property will meet the mortgage payments and operating expenses, plus a little extra for surprises, you will qualify for the loan. If you wish to buy properties and flip them, you must have a realistic budget for necessary expenses until the resale and identify a source for the money to pay those expenses. If the money will come from borrowed funds— because you borrow enough to buy the property and meet the expenses—then your personal lending credit limit does not matter. This concept is at the heart of private individuals' ability to invest in real estate.

What if I make a bad decision?

Almost everyone will make a bad decision at some point. And, while you can never eliminate risk, you can manage it wisely.

Generally speaking, the larger the profit you expect to make on something, the greater the risk will be because there is always a lot of competition for low-risk deals. Everyone wants to find one. If you are buying low-risk property, the competition will drive up the price until your profit is relatively small, which is not necessarily a bad thing. A friend of mine started investing in rental houses twenty-five years ago, in a relatively small town. Today, he owns hundreds of rental houses, three hundred apartment units, a few office buildings, and a retirement community. He now spends all his time fishing and traveling while his son runs the multimillion-dollar business. His success was accomplished with low-risk, low-profit properties and the passage of time.

You can minimize risk in two ways. One is by investing in low-risk properties. Typically this would be something like a brick, single-story rental house with three bedrooms and two bathrooms in a good school district. There is almost no way to get hurt, as long as you pay a price that is consistent with other home sales in the area. Another way to minimize risk is through analysis and knowledge, using the tools in Appendix C.

Finally, always have a Plan B. Ask yourself, "What is the worst thing that can happen," or "What are the ten worst things that can happen?" Once you think of them, you have the ability to create a Plan B for each one—"If Plan A does not work out because of [X], then I will immediately do the following [Plan B]." Thinking of Plan B ahead of time while things are calm guarantees more rational thinking, better solutions, and faster action.

How do I find out more about investing in real estate?

Talk to people you trust, or read general books and articles, to obtain a solid background knowledge. Soon, you will have an idea regarding the type of property you want to purchase for your first investment. Next, read several books about that particular type of property.

You will also need to learn some tax law because many investing decisions are affected by the potential tax consequences. Mastery of some very simple bookkeeping skills is also important. If you plan to be a landlord, you will need to familiarize yourself with the landlord-tenant laws in your state, which are usually available online or from a county law library. You also should know your local market very well—keep track of local news stories regarding business and real estate. Periodically check out what your competitors are doing. And, the more you engage in continuing education, the more successful you will become. As the saying goes, "The harder I work, the luckier I get."

What do I do next?

You read the rest of this book! Do not stop when you reach a chapter that excites you and motivates you to rush out and find the first piece of available property you see. Investing in real estate is a fairly uncomplicated matter, but there are many pieces to the process. Many of the pieces are significant. For example, tax laws can affect what properties you target, how you evaluate what to offer, how you structure the deal with any partners or with your lender, the length of time you plan to own the property, and what you should do before you sell that investment down the line.

Chapter 2

PARTNERS— WORKING WITH OTHERS

■ Should I have a partner?

■ How can a partner help me with influence? Isn't that illegal?

■ Will I always need partners to invest in real estate? Will I be able to go it alone later if I take a partner now?

■ How do I choose the right partner?

■ I do not know anyone who fits my partner profile. How can I find the partner I need?

■ If I decide to find a partner, what should we talk about before we decide to invest in a real estate project together?

■ What things should I discuss with any potential partner if I already have a particular investment property in mind?

■ If one partner wants out after investments are made, do we have to sell everything and split up the cash, even if that means we all lose money?

■ I am afraid a partner might sell his or her shares to someone I cannot work with. How can I protect myself?

■ Should we put our agreements in writing?

■ What are the different ways to structure a partnership?

■ Can I buy some forms and set up my own business entity?

■ What are general and limited partnerships?

■ What is a limited liability company?

■ What is a corporation?

■ Is a Subchapter-S corporation different from a regular corporation?

■ Should all small corporations elect Sub-S status?

■ All I need is someone to cosign a note with me. Do I need a formal partnership or something similar just to have someone cosign a note?

■ How do I choose the best partnership vehicle among all these possibilities?

While you might decide to go into real estate investing on your own, if you have a good understanding of all the ways you can partner with other people to meet your financial goals, you will be even more excited when you read about specific investment opportunities later in this book because you will know they are all attainable. The perspective that everything is possible when you have a partner will make it even more energizing to dream and talk about your plans.

Working with others can be a fun, rewarding way to turn your combined money and talents into incredible returns. In the alternative, it can result in the loss of friends, family, and financial security. The secret is knowing when and how to partner. The first part of this chapter will use the word *partner* in very general terms, indicating two or more people working together toward a common goal. In reality, a *partnership* is a specific legal mechanism for doing that. There are other legal mechanisms as well, such as corporations and limited liability companies, which will be discussed in specific detail later in this chapter.

The decision to have one or more partners should be made before you look at any property. Deciding to have a partner will affect your entire strategy. In addition, if you wait until you are shopping for real estate to think about partners, you will be too caught up in the thrill of the hunt to spend time on partnership details.

Should I have a partner?

I once made the mistake of taking on a partner for the sole reason that he was a friend. I wanted to do him a favor and teach him the business. I thought it would be fun to work together because our families always had a great time together socially. Unfortunately, none of these are rational reasons for having a partner. Anyone could have told me the relationship was doomed from the start, but no one opened their mouth. I learned the hard way. I lost a partner and a very dear friend. Do not fall victim to the same trap.

If you lack something that only a partner can supply, then you should find someone who can fill that gap for you. If the two or more of you can make something better than you can by yourselves, then by all means join forces. If you are just looking for a partnership for the sake of companionship, then things will probably fall apart fairly quickly. Typically, partners bring at least one of the following to the table:

1. money;
2. access to money (borrowing);
3. knowledge;
4. influence; or,
5. time.

How can a partner help me with influence? Isn't that illegal?

We are not talking about bid rigging or insider trading here. The influence that you want a partner to provide is more a matter of credibility regarding a project. If you have no real estate reputation in the community, a partner can give you access to lenders who will actually listen to your proposal and read your analysis. He or she can make introductions to people who routinely buy or sell real estate for their own account. Reputable and reasonably-priced contractors who might not otherwise take a project as small as yours might do so because of your partner and the desire to retain his or her good will. Never underestimate the power of influence. Remember the saying, "It's not what you know, it's who you know." There is a lot of truth in it.

Will I always need partners to invest in real estate? Will I be able to go it alone later if I take a partner now?

As you become a more sophisticated investor, you may want to take on partners simply in order to spread out your risk, which is very common. People who specialize in small apartments might invest money with someone who specializes in retail space, and vice versa. Others who own fast-food locations, office buildings, and convenience stores might enter partnerships with each other. Each person does what he or she does best, but each has diversified his or her investment portfolio into other areas without having to learn everything about the other areas. This way every partner minimizes his or her risk in case there is an economic downturn that affects only his or her specialty.

How do I choose the right partner?

Follow these steps to determine what kind of partner you need.

1. Make a list of all assets and skills you will need for a successful investment. Here are some examples:
   - cash
   - assets
   - borrowing strength
   - time
   - discipline
   - experience
   - energy
   - specialized knowledge
   - connections
   - marketing abilities
   - influence

- focus
- management abilities

2. Which assets and skills do you have already?

3. Which assets and skills can you obtain—through training and research, for example—by yourself? Do not make the mistake of thinking you can learn everything and overcome all your personality strengths and weaknesses.

4. Of the remaining assets and skills you need, which ones can you purchase on the open market, such as apartment management services?

5. Looking over the rest of the assets and skills on the list, which ones are so critically important to success that the project cannot be accomplished at all without them?

The items you list in Step 5 are the assets and skills that you would want one or more partners to bring to the table. Ideally, you should choose people who need you—who cannot or will not do the things you listed in Step 2.

Once you identify the people who have the assets and skills you need, make sure you can work together. It is all right for the brilliant, creative, and highly energetic person to have an extremely organized and unimaginative partner. But, you must each recognize your own limitations and defer to the one who has the strengths. The disorganized partner should not be in charge of the accounting. The methodical one should probably not volunteer to find the deals.

I do not know anyone who fits my partner profile. How can I find the partner I need?

If you are an outgoing person, approach people who are likely to have the things you need. If you need money and organization, then accountants might be the most likely targets. Talk to several about your ideas. People with high incomes are generally looking for good long-term investments. They usually have some cash to invest, sizeable borrowing power, and little time. If you are the one with the money and borrowing power, but little time or experience, ask bankers about small but respected real estate investors who seem to be up-and-coming.

Of course, none of this works if you are uncomfortable approaching strangers. Your first partner may need to be someone who does feel comfortable approaching strangers, and then you can bring in additional partners if you two choose. While you might be splitting the pie more thinly with each additional person, you might not have any pie at all by yourself.

If I decide to find a partner, what should we talk about before we decide to invest in a real estate project together?

In this situation, you are selling yourself and your potential, rather than the merits of any specific investment. You need to have a clear vision of what resources will be necessary for your venture, and who brings each resource to the table. Discuss your strengths, your potential partner's strengths, and how they can complement each other to do better than either of you could do alone.

Agree on a timeline for your first investment and the goals you want to meet with that investment. Make sure your potential partner's financial goals are in line with your own. You should find out if your potential partner's goals consist of making quick cash, especially if your goals are more along the lines of equity growth and future income. This will make a dramatic difference in whether you two decide to become partners at all, and, if you do become partners, what properties you look for.

The timeline also serves as an exit strategy—you will know when your business relationship will end. Failure to purchase an appropriate investment together within the time specified should result in each of you moving on to other separate opportunities, or specifically agreeing to extend your time period together.

Many people who fail at working together as partners never seem to agree on anything because they fail to effectively communicate with each other about these items. One partner eventually gives up on the other, and they quit speaking to each other. The partners never have a specific discussion about ending their working relationship. Eventually, one person does a deal with someone else, while the other partner is left feeling betrayed and used.

What things should I discuss with any potential partner if I already have a particular investment property in mind?

You should talk about the investment opportunity in realistic terms, which includes three possible outcomes of investing in the property: (1) the best case scenario—if everything goes as planned; (2) the most likely scenario—what you can expect under reasonable circumstances; and, (3) the worst case scenario—how bad it will be if your projections are inaccurate. Your discussion should include your budgets for acquisition, improvement, operations, and marketing and sales.

All potential partners should have a clear understanding of your contributions and what they will be expected to add to the venture. If there are surprises—like additional cash requirements—who will supply them and under what circumstances? Additional cash, for example, might be supplied by one partner injecting more money into the deal but taking a larger share of the profits or taking a promissory note. Alternatively, the partner might arrange outside financing and put a second mortgage on the investment property. These things must be discussed in advance.

Finally, you should discuss something called *exit strategy*. What happens if one or more partners wants to withdraw from the investment? You will need some sort of a *buy-sell agreement* so that the remaining partners can buy out the exiting one at a fair price to all. In the absence of a buy-sell agreement, your former partner might sell his or her interest to someone you find objectionable, or someone who does not bring any value to the relationship. It is also common for a partner's departure to trigger huge accounting and legal fees as everyone squabbles over what the partnership interest was worth. This can be avoided with planning.

If one partner wants out after investments are made, do we have to sell everything and split up the cash, even if that means we all lose money?

With some preplanning, you will not have to liquidate your investments simply because one partner wants or needs to exit. That preplanning consists of a buy-sell agreement.

A buy-sell agreement will require the services of an attorney, but it will be money well spent. You can spend a little money on the front end for the agreement, or you can potentially spend thousands of dollars on the back end, fighting with your former partner. At a minimum, the buy-sell agreement should cover how to value each partner's share, payment terms for buying out a partner, whether an exiting partner will be relieved of any responsibilities of the loans they signed, and the circumstances under which a partner can be forced out.

Your buy-sell agreement can specify that the partner who wants to exit can set the price for his or her share. Then, the other partner can decide whether he or she wants to buy or sell at that price. If the price is too high, the exiting partner could be forced to buy and end up owning the entire investment. He or she could then try to sell the entire investment to a third party.

Buy-sell agreements only work if all partners have the ability to buy out the other. If one partner is financially strong and knows the other partner is not, then abuse may occur. The wealthier partner could claim a desire to exit and set a very low price for his or her shares, fairly confident that the other partner could not afford to buy even at the low price. The partner who could not afford to buy would have no choice but to sell his or her share of the business at the artificially low price. This is just one example of why it is a good idea to have a lawyer draft such documents or at least look over one that you have drafted on your own.

I am afraid a partner might sell his or her shares to someone I cannot work with. How can I protect myself?

A buy-sell agreement usually covers this situation. Normally, if it is agreed to in a written buy-sell agreement, an exiting partner must offer his or her shares to the other partners before selling to an outsider.

Should we put our agreements in writing?

Absolutely, positively, and without exception you should put your agreements in writing. Sometimes people are dishonest, but usually, people tend to remember things differently when it is long after the fact. For example, something that seemed completely unimportant on the first day of the partnership might not be remembered two years later when it becomes critical.

I keep all the notes and draft copies of any negotiations. I keep all emails. Many years later, it might be important to say, "Yes, we discussed that, but then we agreed on something different. Here is the third draft of our partnership agreement containing that issue, and then it was omitted in the final agreement." Every single person who has asked my advice about a partnership dispute wished they had kept copies of notes and earlier drafts of documents.

What are the different ways to structure a partnership?

There are several ways to arrange a pooling of talents, resources, and interests. I have been calling all of them a *partnership* in this chapter for the sake of simplicity. The most common options include:

- general partnerships;
- limited partnerships;
- limited liability companies;
- corporations (including Subchapter–S); and,
- trusts, REITS, and TICs, which are common investment vehicles, but not anything that would be selected for use by a beginning investor. You can invest money in them along with other people, but you would not ordinarily set one up yourself.

Can I buy some forms and set up my own business entity?

You have to know a lot of law in order to know all the pros and cons of different ownership entities and how they apply to a particular group's current situation and future goals. You then have to ask the right questions, and the answers might lead you in a different direction than you originally thought. The tax consequences alone could fill an entire three-hundred page book. Please spend the money for professional advice in this area, including that of an accountant.

If you go into a lawyer's office and say, "I need you to set up a corporation for me," the lawyer will do exactly that. Except for the most unusual circumstances, he or she will not ask you if that is the best vehicle considering your financial and tax picture, future plans, estate planning needs, family concerns, risk aversion, and sophistication. Many attorneys are not even capable of giving you advice regarding these matters! They know how to fill in the blanks on some forms correctly, and they know how to answer your questions about items on the forms. Supplying you with planning advice requires much more depth of knowledge. Normally, a tax lawyer and a tax accountant can provide you with the advice you need.

What are general and limited partnerships?

In most states, *partnerships* are simple agreements by two or more people to work together and divide profits. They usually require no formal paperwork, and nothing must be filed in the public records. It is a good idea to have everything in writing, but it usually is not required by law. This is unlike a *corporation*, which must have certain formal documents and must have something on file in a public place as proof that the corporation exists.

A *general partnership* is one in which all partners have equal authority to bind the partnership as a whole. They all have equal liability for partnership debts and obligations. If someone sues a partnership and obtains a judgment, that person can collect all the money from any of the partners individually. A partnership files an information-only tax return, but does not pay any taxes. Each partner reports his or her personal share of income or losses on his or her own individual tax return. Usually, if a partner dies, the partnership automatically terminates. A general partnership enjoys ease of setup and maximum flexibility. It is also the format most likely to cause problems, misunderstandings, and possible financial ruin.

Limited partnerships are considered safer. One or more partners will be designated as general partners. They can make decisions, and they have full liability for debts. The limited partners just invest money. They cannot bind the partnership to any agreements. If the deal is a financial disaster, the limited partners will lose their investment but have no further liability. This arrangement requires formal paperwork. Just like a general partnership, there is an informational tax return only. If a limited partner dies, the partnership does not end. A limited partnership has most of the flexibility of a general partnership and some of the limited liability of a corporation.

What is a limited liability company?

A *limited liability company* (LLC) is a legal entity allowed in many states. It is set up in a manner similar to corporations by filing organizational documents with the state. Management is not as formal as in a corporation, but all members enjoy the same limited liability. These issues should be discussed with an attorney or accountant before deciding to form an LLC.

In some states, LLCs must pay a *franchise tax*, or privilege tax, to the state based on the value of the company's assets. In those states, forming an LLC might not be an appropriate choice for investing in real estate if the asset value is large, because the franchise tax will also be large. Some states limit the franchise taxes if the entity is a family limited liability company.

What is a corporation?

A *corporation* is a legal entity that issues stock in itself. The corporation owns all assets and has all liabilities. Investors purchase stock, which they may sell to others unless there is a specific corporate prohibition against it. The investors have no personal liability for debts unless they sign a formal guarantee agreement with a lender. The corporation has a board of directors, which is responsible for management. The accounting, recordkeeping, and meeting requirements are more stringent than with partnerships. If a shareholder dies, the corporation does not automatically come to an end. Instead, the shareholder's heirs inherit his or her stock, and things continue just like before.

Some small corporations have buy-sell agreements just like partnerships. If a shareholder wants to exit, or becomes incapacitated or dies, the agreement will control what happens to his or her stock.

Is a Subchapter-S corporation different from a regular corporation?

Within some IRS limitations, corporations can decide if they want to be taxed at the corporate level or not. A typical large corporation such as Hewlett-Packard pays taxes on its profits. After paying taxes, it decides how much money it would like to pay to shareholders as dividends. The shareholders then pay taxes on their personal dividends. This is called *double taxation*.

A small corporation might elect something called *Subchapter-S status*. A Subchapter-S corporation (usually called "Sub-S") is simply a tax term. It is not a different kind of corporation, it is just taxed differently. A Sub-S does not pay any taxes on its income. Instead, it reports to the IRS how much of the income or loss should be allocated to each shareholder. The individual shareholders then pay taxes on their shares of the income according to whatever tax bracket they are in.

Should all small corporations elect Sub-S status?

Usually Sub-S status works out to the advantage of the investors. If, however, the corporation needs large cash reserves, or if it reinvests its profits, then the shareholders will have paper profits but no cash. Here is an example of that type of situation when the investment is raw land.

Example:

Revenues	$239,000
– Operating expenses	– $65,000
– Mortgage interest payments	– $94,000
= Taxable income	$80,000
– Revenues for another investment	– $80,000
= Cash left in bank account	$0

In the example, the taxable income was $80,000. If there are two shareholders, each one had a taxable income of $40,000 for a Subchapter-S corporation. But the corporation did not distribute any cash to them because there was no cash left at year end. As a result, the shareholders will have to pay the taxes on $40,000 by using money from other sources instead of from this particular investment.

All I need is someone to cosign a note with me. Do I need a formal partnership or something similar just to have someone cosign a note?

Someone else can lend his or her financial strength to yours in order to assist you in obtaining a loan. That person does not have to be a formal partner or a shareholder in a corporation. If he or she is willing to sign the note without any expectation of sharing in the profits of the venture, then he or she can be a cosigner or a guarantor.

Cosigners have their names at the very top of the promissory note where it says, "John Doe and Jane Smith promise to pay to the order of ...." Cosigners and borrowers are both equally responsible for all payments and the full amount of the loan. The lender reports payment information to the credit bureau for both of them. If John defaults, the lender can sue cosigner Jane immediately and does not have to try to collect the note from John first. Most cosigners believe they are just adding their names so the borrower will qualify for the loan. As a responsible business person, you should educate potential cosigners beforehand, so they can make an informed decision.

Guarantors sign at the end of the document. Their names do not appear on the face of the promissory note. A guarantor agrees that if the primary borrower defaults, the guarantor will pay the loan in full or will make arrangements to cure the default. The lender does not have to attempt collection from the borrower first before going after the guarantor. This arrangement sounds a lot like cosigning, except for the following.

- Lenders report payment information on all cosigners but not on guarantors. The only time credit information would be reported on a guarantor is if the guarantor does not pay when requested to by the lender and the lender has to sue the guarantor.

- Cosigners are on the hook for the entire term of the loan. Guaranties can be limited in many different ways, such as for a certain number of years, for a certain dollar amount, or only after the lender forecloses and tries to collect as much money as possible from the borrower. Any of these limitations have to be written into the guaranty agreement.

How do I choose the best partnership vehicle among all these possibilities?

This decision should be made with the assistance of a legal or accounting professional or a small business advisor. There are many variables regarding your personal goals, your strategies, your partners, and predictions regarding how any of those, or the tax laws, might change in the future.

Chapter 3

FIXER-UPPERS— PROFITING FROM OTHERS' NEGLECT

- I do not have much money and cannot afford expensive repairs. Can I still invest in fixer-uppers?
- How do I find fixer-uppers?
- Are there any government incentives for fixer-uppers?
- I have read about people buying foreclosed houses from HUD as investments. How does that work?
- How much should I pay for a fixer-upper?
- How long will it take to fix up the property?
- How can I minimize my turn-around time on a fixer-upper?
- What are the most common surprises with fixer-uppers?
- How much should I borrow?
- Does the lender give me the money all at once?
- Is any special record keeping required for fixer-uppers?
- What is the difference between buying fixer-uppers and flipping properties?

Many new investors target *fixer-uppers*. They are always good investments, provided you are comfortable calculating potential repair expenses, time to completion, and estimated property values once everything has been finished.

If you are not very handy with a toolbox or estimating repair expenses, this does not prevent you from investing in fixer-uppers. Look for properties in need of simple updating—new carpet, new paint, and some updated landscaping can work wonders. All of those things are very easy to estimate by obtaining quotes from professionals. Plumbers, electricians, and carpenters are different. They will say, "The price depends on what I run into in the way of surprises…" If you are new to this, any conversation that begins with the words "It depends…" and does not give you any guidance regarding what everything depends on should set off alarm bells in your head.

I do not have much money and cannot afford expensive repairs. Can I still invest in fixer-uppers?

The obvious answer is that people who are handy can do their own repairs and upgrades. This is called "sweat equity" because you are usually out on the roof in August, sweating like a mule, doing whatever is necessary. It is not the only route, though.

> **Tip:** You can often secure 125% financing or more to buy a fixer-upper!

The normal rule is that a lender will loan you 75% or 80% of the appraised value of a property or the purchase price, *whichever is less*. In other words, if you are able to buy a $100,000 house for $100,000, the lender will advance you $80,000. If you are able to buy a $200,000 house for $100,000, the lender will advance you the same $80,000 and no more! Experienced investors often obtain better financing terms, simply because of their track record and cred-ibility. This book is written for beginning investors, however, so there is no point in painting a rosy picture that is not going to exist for you.

The exception is when you have a credible plan to increase the value of property through repairs or improvements. It is not enough to say, "I am a brilliant investor and I am buying this house for $100,000 even though the true value is $200,000, so I want 100% financing." That will not work. The lender has no reason to believe you are smarter than the average bear.

Compare that statement with: "I can buy this house for $100,000 and spend $35,000 fixing it up, after which it will be worth $200,000. At a 75% loan-to-value ratio, that would qualify me for a loan of $150,000 once the repairs are completed. I would like to borrow $150,000 to buy the house, make the repairs, and have an extra $15,000 for surprises and to make interest payments until the sale." In this instance, you can obtain 100% financing for the purchase, plus enough money for the repairs. This is explained in more detail below.

How do I find fixer-uppers?

Sometimes you can spot these opportunities just by driving around looking at the exteriors of houses, apartment complexes, or small office buildings. Do they look shabby and in need of repairs? This condition is called *deferred maintenance*. It means that the owner has not maintained the property, made repairs, painted, and/or replaced landscape plants as these things became necessary. Instead, the owner deferred the maintenance—put it off until later in order to save money. While it probably worked in the short run, eventually the property will sell for much less than if it had been properly maintained.

Do not wait for a "For Sale" sign to go up. By that time, you will have a lot of competition for that property as other investors flock to it. Contact the owner, and see if he or she might be interested in selling. You can usually find the owner by making inquiries at the local tax assessor's office. This is called *cold calling*. It is a numbers game. If you ask enough people, some percentage of them will say yes. You cannot get your feelings hurt when most of them say no. Do not waste time trying to persuade the "Noes." Just say, "Can I check back with you in six months or so?" and then go on to the next owner. Remember to check back, though. You will be surprised how often you can plant a seed, and then see it come to fruition six months later.

Other sources for finding fixer-uppers include:

- Elderly property owners who might not have the time, energy, or money to maintain their properties. They might have been planning to sell for several years, but probably have never gotten around to talking to a real estate agent. This is called inertia. It is a principle from physics, and it means that bodies at rest tend to remain at rest. In other words, good old-fashioned procrastination can be your best friend, as long as you are not the one procrastinating.

- Properties in older neighborhoods that are undergoing gentrification. This means that it used to be an undesirable neighborhood, but now young professionals are buying properties and fixing them up in larger and larger numbers. The neighborhood is becoming more desirable. Property values are increasing, but not so rapidly that you cannot easily find real estate at bargain prices.

- Rental properties that seem to have trouble attracting or keeping tenants, even though the general area has high occupancy rates. This is usually a sure sign of an owner who (1) is getting tired of making mortgage and insurance payments on a vacant property; (2) is unwilling or unable to spend the money necessary to attract tenants; and, (3) might view you as a hero if you want to buy it.

- Local, state, and federal governments offer incentives for homeowners, and sometimes even investors, if they will repair properties in economically depressed areas. See the next question for details.

Are there any government incentives for fixer-uppers?

Yes, there are two types of incentives. One is the federal government's *rehabilitation tax credit*. It offers credits that reduce taxes, dollar-for-dollar, for expenses associated with the renovation, rehabilitation, or reconstruction of certain buildings. The credit is 10% of the expenses for buildings placed in service before 1936, and 20% for certified historic structures. In other words, if you spend $30,000 for rehab expenses, you can reduce that year's income taxes by 10% of the $30,000, or $3,000.

Normally, such old structures would not be suitable for a beginning investor. If, on the other hand, you have experience in construction or renovation, this could be a good opportunity. In addition, you can sometimes find such older properties that had a complete plumbing, mechanical, and electrical update within the last ten years, but now need other, more easily estimated, repairs.

State and local governments often provide grants, low-interest loans, and/or discounted purchase prices for investors willing to rehabilitate properties in certain areas. In addition, the U.S. Department of Housing and Urban Development (HUD) offers substantial incentives for investors willing to rehabilitate affordable housing. For more information, download the HUD publication entitled *Best Practices for Effecting the Rehabilitation of Affordable Housing* (September 2006), available at:

www.huduser.org/publications/affhsg/bestpractices.html

I have read about people buying foreclosed houses from HUD as investments. How does that work?

HUD homes are not always fixer-uppers. HUD has many, many homes for sale that are in excellent condition. Those normally sell rather quickly to consumers who want a home of their own, or to investors who desire immediately available rental properties. The dregs, the ones in need of repairs, sometimes offer the best opportunities for investors.

Individuals can buy single-family homes directly from HUD, often at substantial discounts. If you are a real estate broker or licensee registered with HUD, you can also earn a 5% commission if you make that a part of your offer. First priority is given to people buying their own residence. If the property remains unsold for some period of time, it will be made available to investors as well. The HUD asking price will always be the appraised value of the property. During what is called the *offer period*, all potential purchasers make sealed offers. At the end, the one that provides the most net money to HUD is accepted. You do not have to offer the appraised value.

If there are no offers, then the property goes into what is called the *extended period*. Extended period properties have the highest percentage of fixer-uppers. Offers will be accepted on any business day. If one is accepted, the broker will be advised within forty-eight hours.

How much should I pay for a fixer-upper?

You figure out the top purchase price for a fixer-upper by working backward from what you think the property will be worth after your repairs or cosmetic updates. You generally want your total expenses—purchase, repairs, closing costs, and holding costs—to be no more than 80% of the value of the property after you are finished. That is enough of a cushion so that if your estimates are wrong, you probably will not get hurt. The more cheaply you can buy it—under that 80% threshold—the better.

How long will it take to fix up the property?

The time period from purchase to rental or sale depends on how much of the work you can do yourself, how much time you have to do it, how efficiently you can hire and manage contractors, and whether you run into any surprises. If you are inexperienced in making your own repairs, ask trained professionals to give you an estimate of the time involved. Also be sure to ask what their lead time is. A plumber who can complete a job in three weeks is not much use to you if he or she has so much work that you must give six months' notice in order to get on his or her list.

Virtually every new investor I know is of the opinion they can close on a property, make all repairs, and then sell it or receive rental income within six months. Without a great deal of experience and your full-time attention, this would be extremely unusual. You should count on nine months, at a minimum.

How can I minimize my turn-around time on a fixer-upper?

If you are handy, and do not have a full-time day job, doing most of the work yourself will allow you to control the timing.

The next best strategy is to spend the extra money to hire top-notch subcontractors. The larger, established companies will charge more, but its workers will actually show up at the job site on time and with all the materials they need. You run a much higher risk of delays if you try to find the cheapest possible plumber, who has no employees, and who works out of the back of his or her pickup truck. I am not saying this is a poor choice if you know the person or his or her reputation. I am just saying that if you know neither of those things, you are more likely to suffer unpleasant surprises than if you go with a larger company.

The third successful strategy is to minimize time on the market if your strategy depends on resale. Identify the landlords in your marketplace who own multiple properties of the type in which you want to specialize. Usually the local property management firms are good prospects. They will not share with you the names of their clients, but they will tell you if they have clients who want to increase their holdings. If you can develop a pool of buyers who will purchase anything you rehab, then you will not waste any time on marketing and sales activities.

If you plan to buy and improve properties to keep for rental income, you can tap into several pools of always-available tenants. In many communities, Section 8 and other low-income housing is scarce. Eligible renters are able to receive rent vouchers from the government if they can find qualified housing. If you are able to get on the approved list for such housing, you can have a long line of ready tenants each time you complete a rehab. The government pays the rent, the tenants generally take very good care of the property because of their lack of other options, and it is a real win-win situation.

Example: One of my relatives specializes in group housing for developmentally-challenged adults. Two or three adults who have been determined capable of independent living reside in a home together. They receive assistance from a government or privately funded support group. The rent check comes from that support group each month, regular as clockwork. The tenants have always been quiet, regular in their habits, almost obsessively neat and clean in their care of the premises, and very stable. In fact, my relative has had no tenant turnover for many years! As fast as she can buy properties, she can fill them.

Think about these sorts of strategies when investing, and you will improve your odds greatly.

What are the most common surprises with fixer-uppers?

The number one most common surprise is things taking longer than you think. This is either because the scope of the job is larger than you anticipated, or simply because of inexperience in estimating time to completion for various tasks.

Things *always* take longer than you think. Seemingly simple tasks require vast amounts of time. Necessary parts are not available, so everything stops while you go to the store or wait for deliveries, sometimes from far away. One contractor failing to show up for work on the assigned day can have a domino effect, causing other workers to fall behind. They are then forced to fit you in between their other jobs, so they do not fall behind schedule on every other work site.

For example, you must make plumbing repairs before you fix walls, because you often have to tear out walls to get to plumbing. You have to make drywall repairs before you can paint. You must paint before you lay carpet. If your schedule calls for the plumber in Week 1, drywall in Week 2, painters in Week 3, and carpeting in Week 4, you will be dead in the water if the plumber shows up one week late. You will lose your slot for all the workers, who will be working on other jobs during the reassigned week you need them. If the drywall company cannot get back to you for three weeks, everything else stops in the meantime.

The next most common surprise is regarding the expenses involved. This surprise could result from inexperience, such as failing to notice rotting window frames, a roof in need of repairs, or outdated electrical wiring that will have to be brought up to local building code requirements. Or, it could be simple bad luck, such as when you replace inoperable toilets and discover that the entire sanitary sewer line out to the street must be replaced.

The best defenses are:

1. knowledge, gained by reading books devoted to fixer-uppers;

2. pre-purchase inspection reports by trained professionals (which usually cost $300–$500 for a house);

3. avoiding properties more than ten years old, unless you are relatively sophisticated; and,

4. in-depth discussions with repair persons and inspections department personnel regarding common surprises in your area.

The third most common surprise is all the little things you never thought to budget for. Do you need a port-a-potty for workers? How much does it cost to rent a construction dumpster, and how much does each haul cost? What will it cost you for builders' risk insurance during construction? What is the charge for a building/repair permit? Will you be required to have a storm water management plan? How much will power cost you? Commercial power rates are higher than residential rates, and temporary power until you have a certificate of occupancy can be at still higher rates. Have you borrowed enough money to cover the mortgage payments during the repair period, or will that have to come out of your pocket? As always, knowledge is power. Learn as much as you can about this field before jumping in.

How much should I borrow?

Prepare a budget of all your anticipated repair expenses. Add items such as those mentioned in the prior section. Multiply this by 10% and include that figure for contingencies—the surprise expenses. Figure out how long it will take before the property can be resold or rented to a tenant. Whatever that is, add three months to the time unless you have a clearly identified stable of buyers or renters waiting for you. What will your mortgage payments, utilities, and marketing expenses be during that time period? Finally, add the purchase price and closing expenses. If possible, this total figure is how much you should borrow.

Does the lender give me the money all at once?

Most lenders will pay out the loan proceeds a little bit at a time, as you make draw requests. Your interest expense on the new money starts as the lender gives it to you, not from the very beginning of the loan. When shopping for loans, be sure to ask each lender about its funding policy. You want to nail down (no pun intended!) answers to the following questions.

- How often do you fund?
- What fees do you charge for administration of the construction loan?

- What must you have before you fund a draw request?
- What is the maximum time delay between a draw request and the money being deposited in my account?
- Do you require me to match funds on draw requests? In other words, if I have bills totaling $4,000, will you fund $3,000 from the loan and must I pay the other $1,000 myself?
- Do you require any retainage, such as reserving 10% of the loan proceeds until the project is completed?
- Do you have any construction-related requirements, such as having a licensed general contractor in charge of the job?

Some lenders disburse a certain percentage of the loan at pre-defined partial completion points. After the property reaches a specific stage of completion, and after the loan officer inspects the property, the lender will release a percentage of the loan money. This can be a problem if you have contractors who require some payment in advance, if you have workers who must be paid at the end of each week, or if you are unable to obtain accounts with suppliers. In addition, loan officers do not always inspect your site right away just because you need the money. It could be many weeks before you receive any money.

Other lenders will deposit money into your construction account each time you present bills for payment. Some charge a handling fee each time you make a draw request. Find this out in advance.

Is any special record keeping required for fixer-uppers?

You should keep meticulous records if your investment strategy involves fixer-uppers. There are five reasons for this.

1. Some of your rehab expenses can be written off your taxes in the current year.

2. Some of your expenses must be added to your *basis*—your purchase price. This determines your taxable profit when you eventually sell the property—sales price minus basis equals taxable profit—and will also establish what size your depreciation deductions are each year. (*Depreciation* is a percentage of the basis.) The higher your basis, the less the taxable profit and the higher your depreciation deductions. Both of these are very good things.

3. Some of your expenses can be *depreciated*—written off on your taxes—faster than others. This is called *cost allocation depreciation* and is discussed in more detail in the chapter on taxes. It requires excellent records.

4. Many purchases and repairs may come with their own warranties. You will need to know which things have warranties, know the length of the warranty period, and have a copy of the sales ticket or invoice for the work or products. If you plan to keep the property, keep a warranty calendar. A month before each warranty expires, inspect that item to make sure it has no problems. If you plan to sell the property, this is valuable information for the buyer, as some warranties might be transferable.

5. Estimating expenses for future fixer-uppers will become easier and more accurate as you develop your own personal database of information.

What is the difference between buying fixer-uppers

and flipping properties?

The most common flip involves rehabbing a property and increasing its value for a quick sale. That is not the only type, though. People also buy distressed properties and options. On the other hand, not all people who buy fixer-uppers do so in order to resell. For that reason, this chapter is devoted to fixer-uppers in general.

Chapter 4

DISTRESSED PROPERTIES— PROBLEMS CREATE OPPORTUNITIES

- Who are the best investors for distressed properties?
- How do I find properties with owners in crisis?
- I saw a television show that mentioned buying government homes at a 50% discount. How does that work?
- How can I invest in foreclosures?
- Will I be able to assume the current owner's mortgage if I buy property that is threatened with foreclosure?
- How can I flip foreclosures?
- Can I buy at creditor auctions?
- How do I find out about upcoming auctions?
- What are the dangers of buying property at creditor auctions?
- What is the upside of investing in creditor auction properties?
- What kinds of people are good at investing in creditor auction properties?
- How much should I bid at a creditor auction?
- What are stigma properties?
- What are demolition orders?
- Why would I buy property with hazardous waste?
- How can I protect myself if I buy brownfields?
- Can I buy heir properties, or do I have to be one of the heirs?
- Can I buy heir property for bargain prices?
- The late-night infomercials all sell "guaranteed" systems and procedures for investing in real estate tax sales. Is there any substance to this strategy?
- What is an example of a tax sale technicality?
- I do not think I can negotiate with people in financial distress. Is there another way to invest in such properties?

Distressed properties are those with one or more of the following problems.

- The owner must sell quickly because of a crisis, such as a job loss, threatened foreclosure, a divorce, or a local government demolition order.

- The property itself has problems that greatly reduce its value. Examples include fixer-uppers, properties in run-down areas of town, or properties with hazardous waste.

- The property has a bad reputation but no real problems. These are called *stigma properties*. I once bought a $250,000 house built in 1902 for only $150,000 because everyone thought it had major *structural problems*. That was the gossip. My own visual inspection, and the $700 fee for an engineer's report, showed me that the house was as solid as a rock.

- The property is being sold at a creditor auction, such as foreclosures, property tax sales, and IRS lien sales.

- The property has too many owners, making it nearly impossible to negotiate a sale; these include *heir properties*.

Technically speaking, either the property or the owner might be suffering some distress in the event of a distressed property.

Who are the best investors for distressed properties?

The best investors for distressed properties are those people with the time and ability to research all the issues related to making an informed decision. At some point you can make the decision to hire professionals to give you the final go ahead. Before you spend the money, however, you want to be reasonably certain there will be no surprise repairs, no overly expensive waste cleanup, and no creditor claims that will still be good even after you buy a property. These will all be discussed in more detail later.

Having a talent for research and knowing where to look for information is not very common among the general population. If you can do the research, and if you enjoy doing it in pursuit of a goal, then you will find yourself with not very much competition as you hunt for investments in distressed properties.

Investing in these properties also requires a certain amount of self-confidence and the disregard of other people's opinions. You cannot be frightened away by a stigma property, for example, just because everyone thinks it is a bad investment. If you are the kind of person who is sure when you are right, with no second guessing, you will do well. If you are often overcome with doubt, especially when other people contradict you, you might not be emotionally suited to this strategy.

How do I find properties with owners in crisis?

Here is the trick about these properties: Most people who know about looming crises—lawyers, doctors, counselors, and religious leaders—are not allowed to tell anyone. Even if you found out, would you really feel comfortable intruding on someone's problems and offering to buy their property cheaply? Most people cannot do this. Instead, network with the lawyers, doctors, counselors, and religious leaders. Let them know you are prepared to buy properties quickly, with little notice. Make sure they know you buy at discounted prices, but you can close quickly. Leave business cards that include the legend, "I buy properties quickly and quietly."

Many people spend a minimal amount—$100 or so—on signs to plaster everywhere. They say something along the lines of: "Problems? We buy properties quickly and quietly. Call 555-0000." I am not convinced this is an effective strategy, because you are shot-gunning such a large audience. I prefer more targeted advertising, such as an advertisement in the "Want to Buy" classified section of the local newspaper, signs at pawn shops, and a website with good placement when someone searches on "quick cash and [the name of your community]."

I saw a television show that mentioned buying government homes at a 50% discount. How does that work?

The U.S. Department of Housing and Urban Development (HUD) is very interested in rehabilitating neighborhoods that seem to be in decline. As one of the tools in its arsenal, it offers to sell foreclosed houses in its inventory at deep discounts to certain classes of buyers. This is called the *Good Neighbor Next Door Program*. Earlier versions were called *Officer Next Door* and *Teacher Next Door*. Qualified buyers can purchase a HUD home in particular parts of a town for a 50% discount off the list price. In return, the buyer must agree to live in the home as his or her primary residence for at least thirty-six months. At the end of that time, the buyer can convert the home to a rental property or sell it for a profit and buy another qualifying house at the 50% discount. In the alternative, the buyer can simply move some place completely different.

> **Tip:** For more information on this program, go to the HUD webpage at **www.hud.gov/offices/hsg/sfh/reo/goodn/gnnd-abot.cfm**.

While three years is a long time to wait before you can see any rental income, if you have no cash, no credit, and no skill for obtaining partners, you could spend the next three years dreaming about becoming an investor. The time will pass quickly. At the end, you will have a rental property or something you can sell for a large profit. You will have cash and the ability to borrow money. You will have a good credit score. Three years is a very short period of time to invest in your future.

How can I invest in foreclosures?

I actually have an entire book on the subject! It is called *How to Make Money on Foreclosures*, and it contains practical advice about finding such properties, negotiating with owners and lenders, structuring the deal, and what to do afterward.

Aside from general investment educational issues, you must also investigate your state's consumer protection laws related to foreclosures. Your lender should know these laws and be able to give you some resources for details. You might also want to check with the attorney general of your state by asking for someone in the consumer protection division. And, there is always the Internet. Do a search on the name of your state, the word "foreclosure," and some combination of the following words, including the quotation marks where indicated:

- "consumer protection"
- "equity stripping"
- rescission
- cancellation
- disclosure

There are two major areas of concern. Some states require certain disclosures when negotiating with a pre-foreclosure property owner. Some states give the owner the right to cancel a sales contract within certain time limits after signing it. Make sure you comply with your local laws.

In addition, a property owner who sells to you because he or she is faced with foreclosure, but who then files for bankruptcy, may be able to unwind his or her deal with you. This is especially true if he or she lost a significant amount of equity on the transaction, or if he or she accuses you of predatory behavior.

Will I be able to assume the current owner's mortgage if I buy property that is threatened with foreclosure?

Virtually every mortgage in the United States today has something called a *due on sale clause*. It makes the entire loan balance due and immediately payable in full if the property is sold or transferred. Just because a clause gives the lender those rights does not mean the lender will enforce them. Lenders spend a lot of money on advertising and incentives to get people to borrow money. The lender loses money if someone pays off a mortgage early, and then he or she has to find another borrower!

This situation is further complicated by the secondary market. Most loans that originate in one place are packaged with several other loans and sold to investors far away. The investors do not even make loans. If a mortgage paying 7% interest is paid off early, the investor has no choice but to take that money and buy government bonds earning 3% or so. The investor would be happier if the mortgage could be assumed by someone credit-worthy, who would continue making the planned mortgage payments.

The bottom line is, most holders of mortgages have large incentives to work with you. The servicing companies, who work for the larger secondary market investors, are working on obtaining more discretion to negotiate with people for loan assumptions. Both of these things mean it will become easier and easier to simply assume loans in the danger of foreclosure, usually with no down payment and very low closing expenses. Bear in mind, however, that you must make sure there are no other liens on the property. As always, obtain title insurance.

How can I flip foreclosures?

When most people talk about flipping foreclosures, they mean:

1. signing a purchase contract with the owner facing foreclosure so that the lender loses all its equity but at least avoids the bad consequences of a foreclosure; then,

2. working out a deal with the lender to accept less than the full amount due on the loan; then,

3. selling your purchase contract to someone else, with the sales price of the contract itself being pure profit to you; then,

4. the person who bought your purchase contract proceeds to closing and is able to buy property at deep discounts.

These are also called *short sales*. The part that depends on the lender accepting less money—coming up short in the cash department—is the key to the strategy.

The plan requires a lot of legwork, as you track down someone with the authority to accept less than the full payment on the mortgage loan, and then find buyers to purchase your contract. On the upside, it is a way to begin investing with no cash, no credit, no partners, and no need to give up your day job.

Can I buy at creditor auctions?

Creditor auctions are excellent opportunities to buy real estate at bargain prices. A wide variety of creditors sell property at auction in order to collect their money. Some examples include:

- lender foreclosures;
- unpaid property taxes due to the local government;
- IRS and state income tax liens; and,
- persons and companies that win a lawsuit and obtain a money judgment against the defendant, but are unable to collect their money in any other way (these are called *judgment creditors*).

How do I find out about upcoming auctions?

Call or visit the place in your county or parish where deeds are recorded. Ask someone there about the local procedures leading up to a creditor auction. Usually, the creditor must publish a notice in a local newspaper of general circulation in the "Legals" section of the classified ads. This could be the paper you read everyday for the news and sports scores. Or, it could be a specialized legal newspaper devoted to just this sort of thing. Other times, creditors must record something in the real estate records, advising that they will auction the property on a certain date and time. Someone at the courthouse can give you guidance.

What are the dangers of buying property at creditor auctions?

You have all the typical risks associated with buying any property. We will not go into those here, because they vary so much depending on the type of property. There is another risk, however, that can lie hidden and deadly for many years.

A creditor auction could give you title to the real estate, but other liens, mortgages, and claims might still be on the property! In other words, another creditor of the former owner might be able to take the property away from you and pay you nothing. The rules change from state to state, but as a general rule, if any creditor on the following list sells property at any auction, every category above that creditor still has a claim on the property.

1. Person or bank holding liens for real estate taxes

2. Co-owners who did not also owe the debt (including community property claims)

3. Person or bank holding first mortgage

4. Person or bank holding second mortgage

5. Mechanics' and materialmen's liens. These might come before the first or second mortgage, if the work was started or the materials delivered before the mortgage was given.

6. Judgment creditors and general tax liens, depending on the order in which they were recorded. Those recorded earlier than the one holding the auction remain as liens on the property.

Note: The IRS has some super-rights in property. Seek professional advice if you find IRS liens.

IRS liens might also cause trouble unless the creditor followed some very specific procedures regarding giving notice to the IRS or joining the IRS as a party in a judicial foreclosure. Those tax liens might continue against the property unless the proper IRS technicalities are followed. For more information on that subject, call the IRS at 800-829-1040, or go to the IRS webpage at **www.irs.gov/ irm/part5/** and read chapter 12, section 4, for details. Various states might have similar provisions. Check with your state revenue department to find out.

Here is an example of the problems you want to avoid.

Example: Suppose Rocky hears about a foreclosure auction scheduled the next day. He goes to it just to see how things work. He is amazed to discover that a house in his own neighborhood is up for auction, easily worth $185,000. The creditor bids $28,000. No one else is present and there are no other bids. Carried away by the moment, Rocky bids $28,500 and wins! He pays the money, and he owns the house.

However, the first mortgage, of $166,500, is still on the property. That lender will be foreclosing next week, as it turns out. The IRS has a tax lien for $82,000, and last year's property taxes of $4,500 have not yet been paid. Any one of those creditors can take the property away from Rocky. He gets no refund of his $28,500. Rocky is out of luck.

What is the upside of investing in creditor auction properties?

The upside is huge—you could buy valuable real estate for only pennies on the dollar. A lot of people own real estate free and clear without any mortgages. Even if the former owner has something called *redemptory rights*—the ability to reimburse your purchase price plus expenses and interest and reacquire his or her property—you still earn interest at above-market rates. Many, many, investors buy at creditor sales for just this reason. They do not really want the real estate, just the high interest rates earned on their money.

Example: Henry owns a vacant city lot that he inherited from his uncle. It is worth $30,000. Because of health problems, Henry incurred large hospital bills last year that he could not pay. The hospital sued him, took a judgment, and sold the property to you for a mere $4,500. That might be a home-run investment for you! But, depending on state laws, Henry may have a certain time limit to repay you the $4,500, plus any insurance expenses on the property if it had improvements, plus 12% interest on everything. You could have kept your $4,500 in the bank, but it would have earned only 3.5% interest. Investing in these auctions is a good deal for you, even if everybody buys their former property back.

What kinds of people are good at investing in creditor auction properties?

People who are good at researching titles and liens are good investors for these properties. They are able to rule out obvious problems before they spend too much time and money on a potential investment.

No matter how good they are, though, such investors should always obtain a *title commitment* and then a *title policy*. The title commitment costs a minimal amount. It says that a title insurance company will insure the title—guarantee the title is good—if the auction takes place in a manner required by law and if you are the successful bidder. That gives you some comfort that it is okay to bid. The title policy is issued afterward, has an additional charge, and is the actual guarantee. The commitment says only that they *will* guarantee title if certain things happen and if you pay the premium.

You also need to be very organized to invest in creditor auctions. A large number of the properties being sold will be unacceptable because of the size of other liens that stay on the property.

How much should I bid at a creditor auction?

You will have to establish your own personal *profit margin*, just as you would for anything else. But with a creditor auction, you have to factor in some additional risks that might cause you to decrease your normal offering price. Assuming you have title insurance and have no fears in that regard, these are the additional risk factors:

- The former owner could file for bankruptcy, and under some circumstances, prevent you from doing anything with the property until all bankruptcy issues have been resolved. You either eventually get your money back, or you eventually proceed with your plans. That "eventually" part, and how long it can take, are what adds the risk.

- In some states, the former owner and any other of his or her creditors have up to one year after the foreclosure to reimburse you for the money you paid at the auction, plus interest at some legally defined rate, and take the property away from you. This could prevent you from doing anything with the property until the time period expires. While the positive side of this problem was discussed perviously, merely receiving a refund plus interest may not be compatible with your investment goals.

What are stigma properties?

A stigma is something that negatively affects the character or reputation of a person or property. It usually has nothing to do with real value, just with perceived value.

Stigma properties cause some sort of fear in people. Perhaps there was a violent crime committed in the home, and buyers believe the house is bad luck, or something similar. A reputation that a house is haunted can discourage most buyers. According to some studies, a registered sex offender within one-tenth of a mile can reduce local property values by as much as 17.4%, but the values bounce right back when the sex offender moves away.[1]

Once you are sensitive to this subject, you will find stigma properties right and left. The trick is to unemotionally evaluate whether the bad reputation is well-deserved, and analyze the long-lasting effect of the stigma. In other words, if you buy at a low price will you be faced with selling at a low price in the future? Or, will the stigma disappear over time? At the beginning of this chapter, I mentioned my investment that was reputed to have major structural defects, placing it in imminent danger of collapse. That was the stigma. The truth was revealed by a structural engineer's report I ordered before the purchase. That same report also served to erase the stigma when I wanted to resell.

What are demolition orders?

When a structure falls into serious disrepair, it becomes dangerous. The most common reason for disrepair is roof leakage that leads to rotting roof supports and flooring. You might think that your property's condition is your business and no one else's, especially if the property is vacant and has "No Trespassing" signs plastered all over it. However, you would be wrong because your local government is vitally interested in fixing or eliminating such buildings and other improvements. These types of property become breeding places for rats and other vermin, drug-related crime, fire hazards, and secret playgrounds for unsuspecting children. First responders called to the scene for any sort of problem risk their lives entering the properties. The properties cannot be allowed to remain in that condition.

1. Larsen, James E., Kenneth J. Lowrey, and Joseph W. Coleman. (2003) "The Effect of Proximity to a Registered Sex Offender's Residence on Single-Family House Selling Price." *Appraisal Journal.* 71. 253–265.

If the owner does not repair the property to a habitable condition, the city or other local government will order it demolished—a *demolition order*. The owner has a certain period of time to conduct the demolition. If he or she fails to do that, the government will tear down all the unsafe improvements, haul off the debris, and place a lien on the property for those expenses. Many property owners cannot afford to fix their buildings or to pay for the demolition. They will eventually lose everything when the city forecloses its lien.

You, as an investor, can become familiar with your local condemnation and demolition ordinances. Once you know how to obtain early warnings, you can research the properties to see if you would like to buy them. Often, a few hundred or thousand dollars to the owner and a promise to the city to make the repairs will put extremely valuable real estate in your hands.

> **Tip:** Do not confuse this type of condemnation with the eminent domain type. *Eminent domain condemnation* is when the government forces you to sell your property to it so it can use it for community betterment, such as for schools or roads. When asking for advice, be sure to specify that you are interested in unsafe structure condemnations.

Why would I buy property with hazardous waste?

Aside from fear of the actual toxic substances in the soil or water, the fear regarding hazardous waste property is the fear of liability for *remediation*—cleanup. Under federal law, anyone in the chain of title is responsible for cleanup, starting with the first polluter all the way to the innocent current owner. Ironically, that widespread and little understood fear is what makes these such wonderful investment opportunities!

Sometimes the presence of hazardous waste is only a myth—the property is a stigma property. Just because someone operated a dry cleaner at a location for thirty years does not mean they dumped chemicals into the soil at the back door. An environmental engineer can conduct the proper tests to confirm the presence or absence of hazardous waste.

Usually, properties with such reputations do indeed have some toxic substance in the soil or in the groundwater. The property owner often feels helpless, unable to sell the property, and fearful that the federal or local environmental agencies will require him or her to clean up the soil or water. Such people will often pay you to take the property off their hands.

How can I protect myself if I buy brownfields?

Brownfields is another name for real estate with low-level hazardous waste issues—real or perceived. Property with high levels of waste and toxins are called *superfund sites*. Most of those are outside the reach of beginning investors.

Here are the secrets about brownfields that few people understand. If you learn more about them, you can specialize in such properties and quickly build a substantial investment portfolio.

1. Most states have incentive programs for people to buy brownfields and clean them up for redevelopment. Some programs will reimburse you for the entire cost of cleanup, except for a small deductible. Others offer outright grants, tax incentives, or low-interest rate loans.

2. You may have toxic substances, but they may be within permissible levels. In other words, you may not have to do anything to clean up the site.

3. Many times, if the toxic substances are in the soil but not in the groundwater, you can seal them off with a parking lot or concrete building pad and not be required to do anything else.

4. There are many, many methods of remediation. Only one of them involves digging up all the dirt, paying to haul it to a toxic waste disposal site, and then replacing it with clean dirt. There are some very inexpensive clean up methods that involve processes happening over time, as you are using the property. It is important to have an approved plan, and then to implement the plan.

This is an exciting investment field with almost no competition, especially if you can find an engineer or lawyer for a partner. Your partner can supply the technical know-how regarding the legal requirements, and perhaps even some or all of the development money. You supply the time. Everyone wins.

Can I buy heir properties, or do I have to be one of the heirs?

So-called *heir properties* usually consist of real estate that belonged to someone who died without a will. Children and grandchildren could all be co-owners, with various percentages of ownership. In addition, a wide variety of nieces, nephews, cousins, and others might be co-owners. In such situations, it is virtually impossible to get everyone to agree to a sale. That is because at least one person will have a sentimental attachment to the property. Additionally, the sale proceeds would have to be split up into such small portions that it might not be worth anyone's time or trouble to even think about selling. The land might be vacant, or one of the heirs might be living in an old house on the property.

If it were not for a procedure called a *partition*, or *sale for division*, such property would probably remain unused forever or unable to be sold. In virtually all states, any single co-owner can request the court to order a sale of the property. After the sale, the money is split among all owners, according to their percentage of ownership. The one co-owner who requested court action does not have to be one of the original heirs.

Any investor can buy out one of the heirs and become eligible to request a partition. It usually takes very little cash to buy the interest of an heir with a small percentage of ownership. Be aware the some people consider this unethical or at least immoral. It is, however, perfectly legal and often the only solution available when property has many owners who are unable to reach consensus and take any action.

Can I buy heir property for bargain prices?

Normally, the property must be sold for at least its appraised value. You can profit in two ways.

1. You pay pennies on the dollar to buy out another owner's interest, and then file the sale for division lawsuit. Another owner, or a third party, buys the property. You are paid according to your percentage of ownership, not according to how much you paid to obtain it. If you pay $1,000 to buy a one-twelfth interest in a property worth $240,000, you receive $20,000.

2. You can be the successful bidder and buy out the other owners. You might or might not get a bargain price, but you do get a property that was otherwise unattainable.

The late-night infomercials all sell "guaranteed" systems and procedures for investing in real estate tax sales. Is there any substance to this strategy?

Yes, they are excellent investments if you know your state's laws regarding property tax sales and redemption rights. Most of the infomercials sell you fairly inexpensive how-to materials. Their real money comes from various levels of title-clearing services they offer to you after you buy property.

What makes a property tax sale unique is the super-priority given to taxing authorities. If there are competing liens on real estate—mortgages, IRS liens, judgment creditors, and liens for unpaid real estate taxes, the property tax lien always comes first. In other words, a sale under that lien wipes out all the other liens and claims to the property, no matter when they were filed.

That is the upside. The downside is that there are a lot of loopholes and technicalities. None of them are terribly complicated, but it is hard to find out what the rules are so you can follow them. They are different from state to state. I suggest that if you want to follow this strategy, you identify a title insurance company with which you would like to do business. Ask to speak to the lawyer who does the underwriting for tricky issues. That person can give you the education you need, because that person will decide if he or she will issue title insurance to you after you buy.

What is an example of a tax sale technicality?

One of the technicalities in my state is fairly common. If someone explains it, the rule is perfectly understandable. If, however, you read the tax sales statutes, you might never see this rule spelled out, and you would be ignorant of it.

In my state, if I bought property at a tax sale, I would receive a tax certificate. The former owner would have three years to redeem and buy the property back by reimbursing me the purchase price, plus expenses, plus interest at 12% per year. Failure to redeem in three years means I can demand and obtain a tax deed.

If the tax collector did something wrong in the process of sending out notices or selling the property, then the tax sale would be void. I might receive a piece of paper called a deed, but it would be worthless. In my state, the real owners would have another three years to file suit against me, reclaim the property, and reimburse my purchase price, expenses, and interest. Time limits differ among states. If the prior owners do not contest the tax sale within the required time period, then they are forever barred and the property is mine.

Exception: The case authority says that the lawsuit the original owners must file is a lawsuit to have me thrown off the property. The only way they can file that lawsuit is if I am *on* the property. In other words, I must have taken physical possession of the property or left some evidence that I am claiming it as my own. For vacant land, it is usually enough to mow the grass now and then, or chop down some trees, or string some wire from tree to tree to indicate some type of fencing. A dozen or so "No Trespassing" signs with your name and contact information might be sufficient if you also visit the property now and then and have picnics on it or something similar. If there is a structure on the property, you could rent it out to someone and that counts as possession. The statute of limitations starts to run when you take possession, and not before. If you never take possession, you will never obtain clear title.

That is the huge technicality, and it is a pretty common one. Like I said, it is not complicated once someone explains it, but you do need that education.

I do not think I can negotiate with people in financial distress. Is there another way to invest in such properties?

You can wait until the actual foreclosure auction, or afterward, to buy properties. This makes the process much less personal, and helps you make rational, businesslike decisions. Read more about this in the next chapter, "Foreclosures".

Chapter 5

FORECLOSURES— ANOTHER LOW- COST SOURCE OF PROPERTIES

- How does a lender foreclose?
- Can I really buy foreclosure properties at 75% of their appraised value?
- At what point in the process can I bid on foreclosure properties?
- How much should I bid at the auction?
- Does the foreclosure remove all other liens and encumbrances?
- Would you give an example of what happens after foreclosure if there are many different liens on a property?
- Can the former owner take his or her property back after I buy it at the foreclosure auction?
- Is it possible to wait until after foreclosure, and then buy the property directly from the lender?
- If I wait until after foreclosure and buy directly from the lender, does that get rid of the borrower's statutory right of redemption?
- Can I pay a small amount of money and buy out the borrower's statutory right of redemption?
- If I buy foreclosed real estate, will the former lender finance my purchase for me?
- How can I flip foreclosures?

The chapter on distressed properties included advice regarding buying pre-foreclosure properties from the owners. This chapter addresses going to the foreclosure auctions or buying the property after the lender has taken over.

How does a lender foreclose?

Lenders foreclose in one of two ways, usually depending on the state where the property is located. Some states, such as Texas, use something called *deeds of trust* as security for real estate loans. The deed of trust actually transfers legal title to a third party, who is empowered to sell the property if the borrower defaults. These are called *nonjudicial foreclosures* or *power of sale foreclosures*.

In New York and other states, borrowers execute a mortgage, not a deed of trust. Generically, we usually call both of these things *mortgage*, but that is not strictly true. A *mortgage* gives the lender a lien against the property, not actual title. If the borrower defaults, the lender must file a lawsuit in order to foreclose. These are called *judicial foreclosures.*

In a few states, the borrower signs something called a mortgage, but it gives the lender a power of sale. Foreclosure is nonjudicial, but the judicial route is allowed and sometimes preferred if the lender knows it will have a fight over competing claims or other such issues.

> **Tip:** I recommend the RealtyTrac website, at **www.realtytrac.com/foreclosure_laws.asp,** for a listing and description of foreclosure laws in each state.

Can I really buy foreclosure properties at 75% of their appraised value?

That is certainly the myth, and it is true many times, but you cannot count on it. You will always have to do your research and independently calculate value before bidding. Up until recently, it was normal for lenders to loan only 75% or 80% of the value of real estate. If the borrower made payments for a few years, and if the economy did well and prices went up, you could buy foreclosures for much less than current market values. Today, with so many subprime mortgages being given many homeowners have close to 100% financing. It is much more common for them to default very early in the loan, sometimes after less than one year. By the time of the actual foreclosure, the full principal balance of the loan, plus all accrued interest, attorney's fees, and other expenses of foreclosure could be far in excess of the value of the property. Just because a lender starts the bidding at a certain amount does not mean that number is far less than the value of the property.

On the other hand, many lenders will open the bidding at 75% of the appraised value of the real estate, even if the loan balance is much larger. That is because if the lender is the only bidder, it cannot be confident in selling the property for the full amount of the loan, plus all expenses. So, it will not bid that much, because the winning bid amount must be posted as a credit to the loan balance. If the lender bids 100% of the value of the property, paying off the loan in full, it might not be able to resell the real estate for that amount. As a result, it would have to take a loss.

At what point in the process can I bid on foreclosure properties?

With both judicial and nonjudicial foreclosures, there comes a time when the lender may sell the property by auction to the highest bidder. There must be some sort of public notice regarding the date, time, and place of the auction. Local lenders can advise you regarding the common practice in your area. In most circumstances, the mortgage lender bids the highest price, but this is not always the case. Private investors, such as yourself, can bid at those auctions.

> **Tip:** Requirements vary by state. In some, you must pay the entire purchase price that day. Others are more flexible. The RealtyTrac website, **www.realtytrac.com/foreclosure_laws.asp**, does a good job of explaining these differences.

How much should I bid at the auction?

Please review the chapter on distressed properties for guidance on this question.

Does the foreclosure remove all other liens and encumbrances?

This first paragraph is a repeat of a list in the distressed properties chapter. Generally speaking, this is the priority of liens and claims on property. Wherever the foreclosing lender falls on this list, everyone earlier in the list keeps their liens on the property, and everyone later on the list loses their liens. If a lien stays on the property, the holder of that lien can foreclose or sell at auction, take your property away from you, and pay you nothing.

1. Person or bank holding liens for real estate taxes

2. Co-owners who did not also owe the debt (including community property claims)

3. Person or bank holding the first mortgage

4. Person or bank holding the second mortgage

5. Mechanics' and materialmen's liens. These might come before the first or second mortgage, if the work was started or the materials delivered before the mortgage was given.

6. Judgment creditors and general tax liens, depending on the order in which they were recorded. Those recorded earlier than the one holding the auction remain as liens on the property.

Tip: The IRS has some super-rights in property. See the following section about IRS liens for details.

A foreclosure removes everything that happened after that particular mortgage was either executed or recorded. Some states make the signing date of the mortgage the important date. Other states say that if the mortgage is executed on January 1, but not recorded in the real estate records until January 3, and some other lien is recorded on January 2, that other lien has better rights to the property than the mortgage. Any title insurance company can tell you the rules in your state.

Would you give an example of what happens after foreclosure if there are many different liens on a property?

Example: Suppose Breanne lives in a community property state, where spouses automatically have rights to property acquired during the marriage. She buys a house and signs a mortgage with First National in January. In February, she borrows a home equity line of credit from Second National. Then, around the middle of June, she gets married. In September a local department store sues her and obtains a judgment. Breanne does not pay the real estate taxes when they are due in October. On December 15, Second National forecloses, and you buy at the auction.

In most states, your property would still have the First National mortgage on it because that was placed prior to the foreclosing mortgage. The real estate taxes have a super-priority and always stay on property until the taxing authority auctions for its own lien. The IRS lien, which was recorded after Second National, will stay on the property unless Second National gave the required notices of the upcoming foreclosure to the IRS. Every other lien and *encumbrance*—claim—disappears from the property.

This is a very general example. Every state has its own peculiarities. Do not act on any advice regarding this question unless you know exactly what the rules are in the state where the property is located. As always, obtain a title commitment before you bid at the auction, and make sure you receive a title insurance policy afterward. The commitment is not the same thing as a policy. You must take some additional steps, and pay more money, before you have title insurance.

Can the former owner take his or her property back after I buy it at the foreclosure auction?

In some states, the former owner, and others claiming through the owner—such as other creditors, a spouse, or heirs—have what is called a *statutory right of redemption*. The law gives the owner a certain time period to reacquire his or her property by reimbursing you the foreclosure purchase price, plus expenses, plus interest at a rate described in the statute. Foreclosed owners in some states have one year to do this. Other states have shorter time periods, or give the statutory right of redemption only if the purchase price was significantly less than the property value. The RealtyTrac website at **www.realtytrac.com** has this information for each state.

Is it possible to wait until after foreclosure, and then buy the property directly from the lender?

You can do that, provided the lender was the highest bidder at the auction. This is frequently the case, however.

In former days, you would approach the Owned Real Estate (ORE) department of the local bank or savings and loans, and negotiate a purchase of the property. Today, loans originated in your hometown are usually sold to investors with headquarters in other states. Those investors are very large companies with huge bureaucracies. It can be very difficult to find the right person in charge of foreclosed property and then be lucky enough to discover that person has the authority to negotiate a sale. Usually, foreclosed property is listed with a local real estate agent for sale.

Real estate agents who list foreclosed property usually place some sort of banner or other notice over their ad, indicating that the real estate is a foreclosure. That is to generate interest, because most buyers will assume the property is being offered at a bargain price. In actuality, it will be offered at the appraised value. The company will accept any offer that is within a certain percentage of the list price. Those percentages vary among companies. After some period of time—exactly how long is another secret of the trade—they will accept any offer at all. If interested in this method of investing, make low-ball offers on several properties over the course of a year. You might get lucky and have a contract. The worst case is that the dialogue with different real estate agents will give you an excellent education in the field, so you can fine-tune your tactics in the future.

If I wait until after foreclosure and buy directly from the lender, does that get rid of the borrower's statutory right of redemption?

No.

Can I pay a small amount of money and buy out the borrower's statutory right of redemption?

Technically, you can purchase the right of redemption. It does not necessarily mean you can be confident that no one can redeem and take the property back. Depending on the wording of your state laws, many other people besides the former owner might have rights of redemption. If a lien holder who was wiped out in the foreclosure can reimburse you, obtain the property, and then sell it for enough to recoup its redemption price, its lien, plus a profit, it may do so.

If I buy foreclosed real estate, will the former lender finance my purchase for me?

To understand this answer, you have to understand the secondary market system in this country. Today, most loans are originated by a bank, mortgage company, or other local lender. Those loans are then bundled into packages worth tens of millions of dollars, sometimes more. Investors buy packages of loans. Those investors are not lenders.

When a mortgage is foreclosed, the original local lender probably has nothing to do with it anymore. An investor group in another part of the country now owns the real estate. It does not loan money, so it will not finance a purchase for you. That same company is more likely to allow you to assume a mortgage loan before foreclosure, though. That is because its investment depends on all those monthly mortgage payments. It would do almost anything to keep the steady money flow. Knowing this, your best strategy might be to work with owners before a foreclosure, to assume a loan. Reread the chapter on buying distressed properties for guidance.

How can I flip foreclosures?

When most people talk about flipping foreclosures, they mean the strategy discussed in the previous chapter on distressed properties. Otherwise, flipping foreclosure properties after you purchase them is just like flipping any other property except for the possibility of having to wait out any statutory right of redemption periods. To illustrate, consider the following example.

> **Example:** Suppose Harry's house is foreclosed. You buy it at the foreclosure auction for $70,000. The house is worth $100,000. Your state has a one-year statutory right of redemption period, during which Harry can buy his house back for $70,000 plus 12% interest. Do you really think you will be able to sell that house to Rachel in three months for $100,000, if Harry can pay Rachel $70,000 and get it back from her? Of course not.

This is why post-foreclosure flips do not happen so quickly in some states. You can read more about general flipping strategies in the next chapter.

Chapter 6

FLIPPING—YES, IT CAN BE DONE SAFELY!

Flipping is an excellent income strategy if it is done properly. But, if you want to flip properties to get rich quickly, you may encounter financially disastrous problems unless you are a very sophisticated and experienced investor.

What is flipping?

Generally speaking, *flipping* is the practice of buying a piece of property and then selling it quickly at a profit. In real estate, it is most commonly seen in four varieties:

1. Buying a property at a low price because it needs repairs and maintenance, making those repairs, and then selling it for a profit.

2. Buying a property at below market price because the owner is in crisis and needs immediate cash, then taking the time necessary to expose the property to the market (usually four to six months) and then selling it for a profit.

3. Tying up property under a contract for some period of time, and then finding a buyer to purchase your contract from you and go through with closing.

4. Pre-construction flips, in which you sign a purchase contract for a property that will not be built for many months or a year, and then selling your purchase contract when the project is completed and prices have (hopefully) increased dramatically.

How do people flip condos?

There has been a lot of hype in the past few years about condo flipping. In most places, the market has cooled considerably and such flips are no longer practical, but people are still interested.

In the typical condo flip, a developer must obtain some percentage of pre-purchase contracts before his or her lender will release any money for construction. That magic number is usually 50% of the total available units. The developer is willing to presell some units at deep discounts because that is the only way it will receive loan funds. He or she hopes that by the time of completion, prices will have increased so dramatically that there is enough profit in the remaining units to make it all worthwhile.

The pre-purchase buyer also hopes prices will increase dramatically. Buyers will make reservations for one or more units in a condo complex that has not yet started construction, and pay a small amount down for the reservations. These are not options, but enforceable contracts. If the developer builds the project, the pre-purchase buyer must buy the units it reserved. If the developer does not build the project, for any reason, the buyers' reservation fees are refunded.

The condo flipper counts on prices rising dramatically in between the date of the reservation and the date of project completion. He or she can then sell his or her reservations to someone else and make large profits without ever borrowing money, going through with closing, or having ownership.

In a perfect world, this is how condo flipping works.

Example: Carl reserves six units in Beach View Condos, scheduled for construction next year. He pays $5,000 for each reservation. At closing, he will be required to pay the balance of the purchase price for each unit, which is another $145,000. If Carl is lucky, then one year later the condos will be completed. Everyone near and far will want a condo in that area. People will be willing to pay $250,000 for a unit just like the ones on which Carl has reservations. In fact, the developer of Beach View Condos is selling units exactly like Carl's, for $250,000 each!

Carl knows he can sell each of his reservations for $55,000. The buyers will then be entitled to go to closing, pay $145,000 (Carl's reservation price), and receive a deed. The total expense to the new buyer is $200,000, to buy a condo worth $250,000. Carl receives his initial $30,000 investment back ($5,000 each for six reservations) plus a profit of $300,000. Everybody wins, but only as long as there is a hot market for condos. It is like a high stakes game of musical chairs—when the music stops suddenly, someone will be out in the cold. If Carl cannot sell his reservations, he will be required to go through with closing or the developer will sue him.

What is the best kind of flip?

The best kind of flip depends on your personality and resources.

People who are good at doing research regarding property values and repair costs would do well with fixer-uppers and *crisis flips*. This strategy also requires someone who is comfortable with taking risks and has the ability to overcome surprises and obstacles. If you have resources consisting of cash, the ability to borrow, or personal time you can invest, these are also good flips for you. Someone who has a full-time job and a full plate of other responsibilities may not have the time necessary for fixer-uppers. These people should concentrate on crisis flips instead.

People with plenty of time, but little cash or borrowing power and little stomach for risk, would do best with the *options* route. Options can require almost no cash at all, absolutely no need for borrowed funds, and no risk except the loss of the option money. They do require large amounts of time to locate another buyer. Normally, property owners willing to grant options do not want you putting "For Sale" signs on their properties or doing any advertising at all. You will have to track down potential buyers and approach them about their interest in buying. If you are shy, afraid of rejection, or not very good at meeting new people, then option flips are probably not for you.

How can I flip safely?

There are four simple rules for safe flipping.

1. Learn as much as possible about flipping—not just through television shows that show decorating and remodeling decisions, but also through good solid advice about what can go wrong and how to avoid it. Beware of seminars until you have enough background knowledge to separate true value from hype and fluff. Quality varies widely, so be careful.

2. Know your market extremely well, so you can confidently predict future property values.

3. Do not get greedy. Never make snap decisions because you are afraid an opportunity might otherwise disappear.

4. Always, always, always have a Plan B. It is your escape route. Think about what might go wrong, such as a market downturn, unexpected expenses, or an injury that prevents you from working on property yourself. What will you do if something goes wrong? That is your Plan B. If you cannot think of a Plan B that results in you surviving with minimal financial damage, then do not do the deal.

Can I get long-term capital gains tax rates on flipped properties?

Usually you will not be eligible for the cheaper long-term capital gains rates when you flip properties. One reason is the time period of ownership. In order to obtain the beneficial rates, you must hold property for *longer than one year*. That long of a time generally does not happen with a flip unless someone miscalculated.

In addition, people who buy properties with the intention of reselling them are considered *dealers* in the eyes of the IRS. We all, of course, intend to resell our properties eventually, if someone offers us enough money. It comes down to questions of timing with the IRS—how often you buy and sell, how quickly you turn the properties, how much profit you make compared to your other sources of income, and other such issues. There are no hard and fast rules, which is always a little nerve-wracking when dealing with the IRS.

The bad thing about dealers is that the IRS does not allow them many tax advantages given to investors or others. Dealers are not eligible for long-term capital gains. Instead, the IRS considers them as people who sell inventory, just like Wal-Mart. All income is taxed at ordinary income rates. Plus, the dealer will have to pay self-employment taxes on his or her income. Finally, the dealer who sells property and holds the financing will have to declare all the profit in the year of sale and pay taxes on it, even though the actual cash will trickle in over many years. Non-dealers declare income each year of the mortgage payments, and only in proportion to the money they actually receive from the buyer.

The bottom line is, flipping may be a good thing for some people. Too much flipping, however, could cost you important tax benefits. Do not let that discourage you if you are good at it. No tax is 100%—you will still be making a profit.

I heard that buyers of flipped properties sometimes have trouble getting loans, just because it was a flip. Is that true?

Unfortunately, that is true. The Federal Housing Administration (FHA) insures home mortgages, so those loans can be sold to investors. Recently, the FHA has become concerned about wide-spread fraud connected with flipping and artificially inflated prices.

The problem is best shown through an example.

> **Example:** Anne would buy a house for $50,000, and flip to her friend Bob for $100,000. Bob would flip to his cousin Cathy for $150,000, and Cathy would flip to her brother-in-law Dave for $200,000. Each time, a bank loaned 80% of the purchase price. The buyer never paid a down payment because everyone was in the fraud together. Finally, Dave would flip the house to some unsuspecting person. That buyer, his or her lender, and the FHA insurance suffer the losses when the property is foreclosed and brings only $50,000 at the foreclosure sale. Dave splits his $200,000 with all his co-conspirators.

To control this type of fraud, Congress passed a rule that affects everyone who flips real estate, not just the criminals.

Under the rules, FHA will not insure any mortgage loan for a property that has been purchased and then resold within a 90-day period. In addition, if the home has been purchased and resold within a 91- to 180-day period, FHA will require the lender to obtain two appraisals if the second buyer paid twice as much (or more) as the first buyer. As a result, if you try to flip a property more quickly than after 91 days, almost no buyers will qualify for loans. If you buy something for $60,000 and try to sell it for $120,000 within six months of your purchase, the additional appraisal fees will make the loan too expensive for many home buyers. As a result, it is more difficult to find buyers for flipped properties.

What is a realistic time frame for being able to flip properties?

The answer to this question depends on the type of flip you do, how much time you can devote to it, and how much profit you want to make. Most of those questions can be answered by reviewing the chapters devoted to specific types of property strategies—foreclosures, fixer-uppers, and others. To me, the best flipping strategy is one that can be done quickly, for modest profits, but can be repeated as often as you want. Two strategies fit the bill perfectly.

1. Place purchase contracts on under-valued properties, allow yourself a 30-day due diligence period in which you can cancel for any reason, and then find someone to buy your contract at a small profit. You may be much better at finding buyers than the current owner. Everyone wins. If you cannot find a buyer, you cancel the contract. This is fair to the seller only if the property has remained on the market for some period of time. It is unethical to do this in a hot market, tying up property the owner could have sold to someone else.

2. Buy properties cheaply because they need someone to haul out all the junk, clean, and paint the walls before they will bring a decent price. Do all of that relatively quickly and cheaply. Sell immediately at a discount price below the market value. If you could do this once per month and make $5,000 each time, would you do it for a year, or would you stress over one property, trying to make a massive flip profit of $60,000 or more?

Is an option contract a type of flip?

Option contracts are described in the next chapter. They are, indeed, a very low-risk strategy for flipping properties. I have devoted a separate chapter to the subject because it has its own technicalities that raise many separate questions. In addition, people other than flippers use option contracts.

What book do you recommend for more information?

Thank you for asking. You were sure I had a book on this topic, weren't you? It is due out in early 2008 and is called *The House Flipping Answer Book*.

Chapter 7

OPTIONS— LOW-RISK FLIPPING

- What is an option?
- If a seller agrees to give me an option to buy his or her property, can I require that the money I pay for the option be used as a credit against the purchase price?
- I know a rich developer who options property for purchase all the time. Why would someone with all that money use options?
- How can I use options in the same way rich developers do, but on a smaller scale?
- If it is such a great idea to tie up multiple properties with options until you can amass enough square footage to make the land more valuable, why don't developers all do that? How is there any room for me to use this strategy?
- Is an option the same thing as a lease option?
- Is an option the same thing as a right of first refusal?
- Are there any technicalities to an option contract?
- How much should I pay for an option?
- How can I avoid two sets of closing costs?
- Where can I find an option contract form?
- What happens if I cannot find a buyer for the property?
- Why wouldn't a potential buyer simply wait until my option expires, and then buy the property at the cheaper price?
- What kinds of property are appropriate for option contracts?

Most real estate investors have used options at one time or another in their careers. They are an excellent tool for minimizing risk while giving you time to see if you can put a deal together.

What is an option?

An *option* is a contract. An owner of land (called the *optionor*) agrees to sell his or her land to a particular buyer (called the *optionee*) for a predetermined price. The optionee/buyer is not obligated to buy, though. He or she holds all the cards. The optionor/seller *must* sell if the other party demands it. The optionee/buyer does not have to buy, no matter how much the owner wants that to happen. The buyer makes no promises at all.

Because of technicalities having to do with contract law theories, the *optionee* (potential purchaser) must pay a fee to the optionor/seller in order to make the option contract enforceable. The fee does not have to be in any particular amount or any proportion to the ultimate purchase price. It just has to be an amount the owner finds acceptable. The fee pays only for the option. It does not pay for the property, nor is it *earnest money* or a down payment.

If a seller agrees to give me an option to buy his or her property, can I require that the money I pay for the option be used as a credit against the purchase price?

No, what you are describing is *earnest money*. If you try to make the money you pay for the option refundable or capable of being applied against the purchase price, then you do not have an enforceable option contract. Do not try to figure out any way to get around this! If you are serious about using options to invest, then be serious about making sure you can enforce them when the seller finds out his or her property is much more valuable than he or she originally thought.

This is how a typical option works.

Example: Stephen owns ten acres of land in an area that is growing rapidly. Melinda knows that Stephen would sell if he could receive $44,000 an acre, or a total of $440,000. She thinks the land would make a terrific small subdivision, but she has three problems: (1) no cash for a down payment; (2) no ability to borrow money for purchase and then development; and, (3) no experience building subdivisions.

It is May, though, and Stephen would like some extra cash so he can go on vacation. Melinda says to Stephen:

1. I will pay you $2,500 if you will sign a contract giving me the right to buy your property any time during the next six months for $440,000.

2. The $2,500 is yours to keep, no matter what happens.

3. But, you are not allowed to change your mind about selling, refund the $2,500, and cancel the contract.

4. If I decide not to buy, I will have no obligation to you, but you keep the $2,500.

If Stephen agrees, Melinda will have six months to use her superior contacts, knowledge, and hard work to find a buyer willing to pay the more realistic fair market value of $66,000 an acre, or $660,000. At the end, she will make $220,000 on a cash investment of only $2,500! Of course, she might not be able to pull it off. If she fails, she has lost her $2,500, but no more.

This type of risk can be managed easily by most people.

I know a rich developer who options property for purchase all the time. Why would someone with all that money use options?

There are two primary risks that an option controls. One is the risk that the purchaser will not be able to find another buyer at a higher price. The option lets the purchaser tie up the property with little or no cash while he or she hunts for a buyer.

The second risk is the danger that a developer will not be able to buy enough properties for a deal. A friend of mine recently purchased sixty-two parcels of land in order to bulldoze the World War II–era houses and build a shopping center. If five or six people had refused to sell for any price, the entire project would have been impossible.

Rather than spend the money to buy fifty-seven parcels and then find out that five other owners had the power to kill his deal, my friend optioned all the properties, one by one. When he knew he had a viable project that could go forward, no matter what some hold-outs might decide, my friend closed on all the optioned real estate. If it had been necessary to walk away and abandon the venture, he would have been out the $100,000 or so it cost to buy the options, but no more. That is a lot of money to you or me, but it was small potatoes compared to the potential multimillion dollar profit on the shopping center development.

How can I use options in the same way rich developers do, but on a smaller scale?

I am going to give an example of using options in regard to heir properties.

Example: The *heir property* strategy usually comes into play when a developer wishes to buy several small parcels of land

and join them together into something larger and much more valuable. This is called an *assemblage*. A lot 52 feet wide and 105 feet deep is not very valuable—you cannot do much with it. That seriously depresses the appraised value. In my town, such a parcel of land near downtown might be worth around $3.50 a square foot, or $19,110. What if you could buy eight of them, though, all next to each other? You would have an acre of land. An acre of land, in the same part of town, would sell for $21 a square foot. Assuming you could buy for $3.50 a foot and sell for $21 a foot, your profit is $764,400!

The trick is, how do you tie up eight parcels of land? With options, of course. The cost to purchase options on those eight parcels would probably be around $500 each, at the most. You spend $4,000 optioning the properties, find a developer who wants to build a small apartment complex or an office building, and sell the land to him or her.

If it is such a great idea to tie up multiple properties with options until you can amass enough square footage to make the land more valuable, why don't developers all do that? How is there any room for me to use this strategy?

Developers are usually not patient people—they tend to think in large dollar increments, and they are typically well known around town. This means they are not going to spend the time looking for and negotiating options on several small lots. Even if they did, the owners would get wind that something was in the air because of knowing the developer by reputation, and they would raise their prices dramatically. My friend who put together the sixty-two parcels is an exception to my comment about patience, and he had to work through straw men.

Rather than spend all the time necessary to find such deals, developers are usually willing to let people like you do it for them. Everyone in the entire food chain, from giant shopping centers down to one-acre parcels for neighborhood office buildings, depends on people like you to spend the time, energy, and effort to bring them deals.

Is an option the same thing as a lease option?

A *lease option* is a specialized type of option. It gives a tenant the right to buy the leased property at some time in the future, usually for a predetermined amount. Sometimes all rent payments will be credited toward the purchase price, and other times they will not. This is entirely a matter of negotiation between the parties. In most states, if the option is contained within the lease or a renewal lease, then the tenant does not have to pay a separate fee for the option. But, if an existing tenant is given an option, then usually the tenant must pay a separate fee to make the option enforceable.

As an investor, you might want to sell rental properties to your tenants under a lease option. In some states, this is an excellent way to manage potential tenant/buyer default without going through all the time and trouble of a foreclosure—you simply terminate the lease, and that is the end of it. In other states, tenants with lease options are given many of the same protections as mortgage borrowers. Be sure to consult with a local attorney before entering into such a relationship.

Is an option the same thing as a right of first refusal?

No, an option is completely different from a *right of first refusal*. With an option, the seller *must* sell if you decide to buy. In a right of first refusal, the owner must give you the first chance to buy the property, but *only* if the owner decides to sell. If the owner decides to keep his or her property, there is nothing you can do to force a sale. In an option situation, you have all the power. In a right of first refusal situation, the owner has all the power.

Are there any technicalities to an option contract?

In most states, there are three requirements for an enforceable option contract.

1. The contract must be in writing and signed by the property owner.

2. The contract must have a specific description of the property and a predetermined method of calculating the sales price (an agreed-upon amount, a certain figure per acre or per square foot, etc.).

3. You must pay something to the property owner for the option contract itself. You cannot get credit for it at closing, as if it were earnest money. If you even suggest such a thing in the option contract, the whole arrangement could be unenforceable.

How much should I pay for an option?

How much you pay for an option will depend on (1) the lowest amount the owner will accept, and (2) the largest amount you can afford to gamble if you cannot find a lender or another buyer. Remember, the money is not refundable.

How can I avoid two sets of closing costs?

Many times, option holders will find another buyer and then have two simultaneous closings—the owner to the option holder, and then the option holder to the new buyer. This is very expensive and inefficient.

The better way is to put a clause in the option contract giving you the right to assign it to someone else, if you choose. That person then goes through with closing with the owner. In the example at the beginning of this chapter, Melinda paid $2,500 for an option on ten acres of land. With an assignment clause, she could then sell her option to someone else for $220,000. That person would then have the right to buy the real estate from Stephen for $440,000, or a total cash outlay of $660,000. There is only one closing, one set of closing costs, and Melinda is never even in the chain of title. This is important if Melinda has creditors trying to seize any real estate she might own.

Where can I find an option contract form?

You should consult with a local attorney. State laws vary widely, so I do not recommend using a generic form from the Internet. On the other hand, U.S. Legal Forms, at **www.uslegalforms.com**, will sell you state-specific forms and give you a free preview so you can decide if the form is what you really need.

What happens if I cannot find a buyer for the property?

If you do not go through with the purchase, you lose the money you paid to buy the option. That is all—nothing worse happens to you.

Why wouldn't a potential buyer simply wait until my option expires, and then buy the property at the cheaper price?

It is always a possibility that a buyer will go around you, find out the details of your arrangement, and then simply wait you out. There is no foolproof way to keep this from happening. As a practical matter, though, it is very rare. Out-of-town buyers simply do not have the time or contacts to do this. Local buyers either want to preserve their honorable reputation, or you already know to avoid them because they are unethical. If you have a good relationship with the owner, and stay in close contact with him or her, then he or she will usually tell you if something fishy starts happening.

What kinds of property are appropriate for option contracts?

Any kind of property can be purchased on an option contract. The next section of this book addresses questions specific to a wide variety of real estate.

Chapter 8

RENTAL HOUSES—THE MOST COMMON STRATEGY FOR BEGINNING INVESTORS

- What is the easiest way to find acceptable rental homes to buy?
- What is the best kind of rental house to buy?
- How much should I pay for a rental house?
- How much will tax savings help me with negative cash flow?
- How do I find good tenants?
- How do I maintain good relations with my tenants while also protecting my investment?
- Who mows the lawn and other such things?
- Do I need any special type of lease for a rental residence?
- Do I have to learn a lot of Fair Housing and other laws so I will not accidentally do something wrong?
- What are some of the pros and cons of investing in rental houses?
- If I want to invest in condominium units, do I follow the same advice as for rental houses?

Single-family residences are the most common type of investment for those new to the field. They are also the most popular for those who desire supplemental income with the smallest risk and least problems. The questions in this chapter are specific to rental houses.

What is the easiest way to find acceptable rental homes to buy?

There are many different strategies for finding these properties. Many are the same as other real estate investments and are covered in other chapters. The easiest way to find a *rental house* to buy is to keep track of homes for sale in your neighborhood and surrounding area. You already know the locale and the relative stability of prices. Management will be easy because you are nearby. You may know the house and its upkeep by reputation.

A word of caution, though. If you know the seller, think long and hard about revealing your identity if you plan to make a low offer. You might want to work through an agent, as an anonymous buyer. A neighbor who has heard you talk often about a burning desire to invest in real estate is a neighbor who might think you are the more motivated party. That person will be the one to stand firm on his or her price, thinking you will be the one to crumble in the end.

Notice when the first "For Sale" sign goes up on each sale home. Most listing contracts expire after six months if they are not renewed. After five months and two weeks, call and request information about the house. At that point, the seller is probably very motivated. You can usually buy the property at a significant discount.

Re-read the chapter devoted to fixer-uppers. You will be able to find many bargain properties with that type of focus. Often, a very minor amount of cleaning, painting, and simple repairs will be enough to make a house rentable.

What is the best kind of rental house to buy?

As a general matter, the best kind of home to buy is usually going to be the current owner's personal residence. Owner-occupants take better care of property than tenants or landlords. You will still need an inspection, but the odds are much greater that the home will have few problems and that maintenance has been performed in a good manner.

Aside from that, you want to find something that is as maintenance-free as possible. For most people, that spells out B-O-R-I-N-G, but you should look for excitement someplace else. The best purchase will be a three-bedroom, two-bathroom, one-story brick house with no large trees, no fireplace, a level lot and a fenced-in backyard. It should be in a good elementary school zone, because younger families are the more likely tenant candidates and those tenants are your best buyers if you ever decide to sell. This is called the *grow your own buyer* strategy.

Wall-to-wall carpet is better than hardwood floors, because you can clean carpet or replace it fairly cheaply. When those hardwood floors are ruined, the price tag is expensive. A fenced-in backyard makes the house seem more safe.

A level lot is easier to maintain—smaller trees do not drop branches on your rooftop, and the absence of a fireplace cuts down on fire risks. Laminated countertops are better than tile because you can replace laminate easily, if you need, but that tile grout will never be white again. For the same reason, look for solid vinyl tub surrounds and sheet vinyl flooring in the kitchen and bathrooms. Remember, you are not buying your personal dream home. People who rent houses are much more flexible in their desires than people who buy homes. Nothing is ideal, but try to buy as close to these recommendations as possible.

How much should I pay for a rental house?

There is a saying in the real estate business that an owner-occupant will always pay a higher price than an investor. When buying rental houses, this translates to the fact that someone who wants to live in a home will usually outbid you if it is a tight housing market. If there are more homes on the market than buyers, you can pick and choose. A situation with many buyers and few homes means you will probably have to concentrate on fixer-uppers. Most potential owner-occupants lack the vision to see through a mess of a property to what it could be with very little effort. You will have little competition for those homes.

Many, many real estate gurus tell you it is all right to buy something with mortgage payments larger than the potential rental income because the property will increase in value over time while your mortgage payments remain constant. They also tell you that the tax write-offs will make up for the *negative cash flow* and you will be rich in the end. It sounds good, we all want to believe it, and it sells tickets to seminars because we are all hoping it is true. Our job would be so much easier if we could pay too much for a property and have everything turn out okay. It is preposterous, though!

If you have negative cash flow, or you must take personal income from your job or other sources to supplement the rental income from the home, how many of those deals can you do? Try to *make it up on volume*, and you will invest yourself right into bankruptcy!

Appendix C has a mortgage payment calculator you can copy into a Microsoft Excel® spreadsheet. If you enter the monthly payment you can afford, the spreadsheet will tell you how much money you can borrow to make that monthly payment.

Read the chapter regarding rental rates and security deposits. Research rental rates in the area for the type of house you want to buy. That is the gross monthly income you will have. Subtract the following numbers. These are my examples, but the percentages might be higher or lower in your area and for your type of property.

- 5% for maintenance and repairs
- 5% for marketing and advertising
- 5% for accounting, legal, and business license
- An estimated monthly amount for insurance and real estate taxes
- Whatever percentage the local government charges for a rental tax, if any

The number that remains is the mortgage payment you can afford. Plug that into the spreadsheet you created, and you will see how much debt you can afford.

Example: Suppose the going rate for a three-bedroom, two-bathroom home in a good school zone is $1,600 per month. An insurance agent told us the annual insurance premium would be around $2,000. The county tax assessor told us the real estate taxes will be approximately $1,600 per year. That is twice what our own taxes are, but homeowners usually receive significant discounts on their property taxes. Investors do not enjoy such breaks.
Here are the calculations:

$1,600 monthly rent
– $80 maintenance and repairs
– $80 marketing and advertising
– $80 accounting, legal, and business license
– $167 insurance
– $134 property taxes
<u>– $18 for 1% rental tax</u>
= $1,041 available for mortgage payments

Using the calculator, $1,041 will make the mortgage payments on a 30-year mortgage at 7.5% interest for a loan amount of $148,881. If you can afford a 20% down payment, that works out to a maximum purchase price of $186,101. (**Note:** Divide the loan principal amount by 0.80 to arrive at this answer.)

How much will tax savings help me with negative cash flow?

First, you need to understand that the government limits how much your rental property deductions can reduce your taxes on other income. There are more details in the taxes chapter under questions about the passive activity rules. As a general rule, individuals can shelter only $12,500 of their other income through rental property tax deductions. Married persons can shelter up to $25,000. In other words, losses on your rental property, including paper losses like depreciation, can save you $4,375 per year in taxes if you are single and in the highest—35%—tax bracket. Married persons can save $8,750 per year in taxes, at the most. Your exact savings will depend on your tax bracket.

The real estate gurus do not tell you about the passive activity rules. They also do not tell you that if you calculate your budget too closely, so that every penny counts, you might suffer catastrophe if your property remains vacant for just a month or two.

For example, let us look back to the example in the previous question. You have $1,041 available each month for mortgage payments. Suppose you want to pay a higher price for a rental house, or have a smaller down payment. Suppose your mortgage payments are now $1,341 per month. That additional $300 per month will take away almost all your tax savings. If the house sits vacant for only one month while you try to find a tenant, you will lose money that year. Can you afford that?

How do I find good tenants?

This question is common to many investment properties. It will be covered in the chapter on tenant selection.

How do I maintain good relations with my tenants while also protecting my investment?

This question is common to many investment properties. It will be covered in the chapter on property management.

Who mows the lawn and other such things?

Lawn care is a matter of preference, and you specify this in your lease. How much trouble will it be for you to mow the lawn once a week in the growing season? Are there shrubberies and flower beds to be maintained? If you leave these matters to the tenant, you will need to inspect the property at least once a month to make sure these tasks are being done properly. In addition, your lease should have a clause regarding consequences if the tenant does not live up to his or her upkeep responsibilities. Most landlords reserve the right to do lawn care themselves, or hire someone else, and charge the tenant a large fee.

For areas with snow, cleaning sidewalks and driveways should be the tenant's chores. In my part of the country, we do not have freezing weather enough days of the year to justify spending the money to freeze-proof all pipes. Instead, landlords contact tenants when temperatures are expected to drop during the night and advise them to turn on the water to a steady trickle. Under their leases, tenants must pay for freeze damage if they fail to follow these instructions.

Do I need any special type of lease for a rental residence?

Many states have specific laws protecting consumer tenants. Some passed a version of the *Uniform Residential Landlord Tenant Act*. Others have similar laws. Depending on the state, there are differing requirements regarding security deposits, required notices before entering the premises, and remedies when the rent is late or the lease is in default. Quite a few prohibit you from having a clause in your lease allowing the recovery of attorney's fees if the tenant defaults. A court can award you attorney's fees, but you are not allowed to put it in the contract.

Your best strategy is to hire a lawyer to draft a lease for you. Call the local courthouse and ask who files the most eviction lawsuits in your county or parish. That lawyer probably already has a good lease written for one of his or her larger clients. You may be able to get a discounted price for your own lease because most of the work is on the computer already. Always ask in advance how much the fee will be. An experienced landlord attorney can tell you that. A novice who needs to learn the subject on your nickel will be unable to give you an estimate.

Do I have to learn a lot of Fair Housing and other laws so I will not accidentally do something wrong?

There are a number of protections for consumer tenants. You should read the chapter on tenants' rights for details.

What are some of the pros and cons of investing in rental houses?

Pros:

- many choices of properties to buy
- typically steady supply of renters
- most repairs and maintenance are easy
- management not complicated
- easy to sell when desired

Cons:

- usually short-term leases of one year
- vacancies have high impact
- can be difficult to place with management company
- consumer protection statutes must be mastered

If I want to invest in condominium units, do I follow the same advice as for rental houses?

For the most part, many of the considerations for buying rental houses will be the same for condos. The next chapter provides additional information that is unique to condominium investments.

Chapter 9

CONDOS—NO-HASSLE OWNERSHIP

- I'm more interesting in flipping condos than holding them for rental income. How can I do that?
- Are there any extra financial considerations I should keep in mind when buying a condo?
- Do condo ownership dues increase every year?
- What surprise expenses should concern me as a condo investor?
- How do I protect myself against surprise expenses?
- Someone told me their condo association charges an "impact fee" for all units with tenants and a separate move-in and move-out fee. Is that legal?
- Can I be held responsible for my tenant's actions in a condominium?
- What is the ideal condo investment?
- After I have several rental houses or condos, does it make sense to sell them and "trade up" to an apartment complex?

Investing in condominiums is kind of like buying apartments one at a time. You enjoy many of the benefits of community management and maintenance, but without having to buy the entire complex. Investing in condominium projects for rental income can be very efficient and profitable, especially if you already own a condo.

You should buy and read a good general book about buying condo units. Even if not pitched to a landlord audience, such books can alert you to many issues you should bear in mind when investing. It just so happens that I have written such a book, called *How to Buy a Condominium or Townhouse*.

I'm more interesting in flipping condos than holding them for rental income. How can I do that?

Read the chapter on flipping, especially the questions about condo flipping. As currently practiced, I do not recommend condo flipping for new investors. The practice depends on a rapidly rising market with ever-increasing prices. Many people are lucky and make a lot of money at it. A large number of others file for bankruptcy because they run out of luck. If your investment strategy depends on luck or on timing the market, you should switch to gambling or day trading.

Are there any extra financial considerations I should keep in mind when buying a condo?

In addition to the monthly mortgage, insurance, and tax payments, you will also have condo association dues. Some portion of that expense is offset by the fact that your maintenance expenses will be less because the condo association will take care of all exterior maintenance and repairs. In addition, your monthly insurance premium should be lower than it would be for a house because you are insuring only the interior of your unit, instead of the entire structure.

People are more likely to invest in condos in another city than they are to invest in rental homes in another community. If that describes you, then remember that expenses can be dramatically higher than they are where you live. Condos on or near the beach, for example, might have insurance premiums five to ten times greater than the ones in your hometown. Property taxes in Florida, for example, can seem extreme to outsiders. Make no assumptions about any of the costs of ownership, but obtain quotes from locals.

Do condo ownership dues increase every year?

Well-run condo associations increase their dues every year. That is because all the insurance, tax, and maintenance expenses also increase. The money to pay those bills must come from somewhere. A condo association that does not have annual dues increases usually trims the quality of goods and services or allows maintenance to go unattended.

The annual dues increases might not coincide with the renewal dates on your tenant leases. In other words, your rent could be calculated based on dues of $150 per month, but those same dues might increase to $300 per month during the middle of your tenant's term. You can either absorb the extra expense, or have a lease clause increasing the tenant's rent if the dues go up. I prefer the second option.

What surprise expenses should concern me as a condo investor?

There are two types of surprise expenses that can alter your investment picture. One was used as an example in the previous question—monthly dues that double with little or no notice.

The condo association establishes the dues each year. Depending on the mix of owner-occupants versus investors, the group with the most votes may take actions antagonistic to the interests of the other group. Owner-occupants might be willing to spend an additional $150 per month for dues in return for a night patrol person, new landscaping plants, and free line dancing lessons on Friday nights. You, as a land-lord, probably do not care one iota about those things, but you have to pay your fair share of the expenses because you were outvoted.

> **Tip:** When choosing investment condos, try to find some in buildings with high concentrations of investors. You will find a lot of sympathetic ears at association meetings, and can reasonably count on some commonality of goals and interests, with a minimum of surprises.

The other condo expense that can completely change your financial picture is a *special assessment*. Do not let the name fool you—condo associations can make assessments many times, for many different things.

A project that does not charge enough in monthly dues to pay for routine maintenance will put off those matters until things become critical. At that point, there will be a very large bill that must be paid. It could be to replace the roof, repave the parking lot, or paint the exteriors of all buildings. All previous owners will have escaped with low monthly dues. If you are a recent purchaser, you will bear the burden of that lack of foresight and find yourself stuck with a large assessment. There is no way to pass this along to your current tenant. You will have to pay it yourself.

How do I protect myself against surprise expenses?

The best way to protect yourself is to be sensitive to the warning signs of potential future surprises. Ask yourself these questions when buying a unit.

- How do the monthly dues compare to other buildings in the area? If they are lower than others, is there a reasonable explanation that does not involve cutting expenses to the bone?

- Examine the balance sheet for the condo association. Is there a healthy bank account to cover unforeseen repairs and a reserve account with steady savings for big-ticket items like a new roof?

- Are there any unpaid bills that seem to be older than thirty days? If such bills appear on the balance sheet, the association may have problems with cash flow. That is usually a sure sign that a dues increase is in the future.

- As long as you are looking at the balance sheet, also look at the "receivables" account. Is there a large number for "dues receivable"? Owners are supposed to pay their dues on the first of each month. Unpaid dues show up in the receivables entry. A large figure in receivables can mean a dues increase, because the money has to come from some source to pay the bills.

- Ask for the monthly profit and loss statements for the last two years. Is the association running at a deficit every month? Are there large expenses for legal fees? Are the actual repair expenses fairly close to the budgeted numbers or not? All of these things can tip you off to potential trouble.

Someone told me their condo association charges an "impact fee" for all units with tenants and a separate move-in and move-out fee. Is that legal?

This practice is becoming more and more common. It is legal as long as the condo documents—the *bylaws* and the *Covenants, Conditions &*

Restrictions (CC&Rs)—allow it. Fees such as these are intended to discourage absentee landlords. You will have to review the documents I mentioned for the presence of any such fees before you buy. You might also want to read minutes of the condo association meetings for the last year or so. This will alert you in case there is a move to amend the CC&Rs and introduce such landlord-unfriendly fees.

Can I be held responsible for my tenant's actions in a condominium?

You should be very careful about tenant selection when investing in condo units. You, as the owner, are the one responsible for complying with all rules and regulations. Failure to follow the rules can result in fines, some of them daily fines that quickly add up to hundreds or thousands of dollars.

Protect yourself by knowing all the rules, checking tenant compliance often, and staying in touch with the local association in case there are any complaints against your renters. Attach a copy of all rules to your leases, and make your tenants responsible for following the rules or paying you a fine.

What is the ideal condo investment?

Personally, I would like to own several condos in a project that is well-located and well-maintained—a place I would like to live for many, many years. I would have several different sizes of condos, with varying numbers of bedrooms. As my space needs change over my lifetime, I could simply move from condo to condo in the same project and rent out any that I am not occupying.

However, the perfect condo investment will depend on your goals. Prime locations will hold their value over time. Because condo tenants are typically younger adults, and condo owners are typically persons with no children in the household, school zones are not quite so important as with a rental house. Pay more attention to local recreational, shopping, dining, and transportation amenities. Close proximity to those things will generally translate to stable and ever-increasing property values.

After I have several rental houses or condos, does it make sense to sell them and "trade up" to an apartment complex?

For many investors, the next logical step after acquiring five or ten rental houses is to liquidate them and buy an apartment complex. Even if you want to keep those individual units, you can still refinance them as a package, pull out significant equity—tax free—and use that money as a down payment on an apartment complex. Apartments give you important economies of scale and savings in your time and money. In addition, there is always a ready market of buyers for apartments, because lenders like a significant portion of their loan portfolios to be in multi-family housing.

The next chapter will answer more of your questions about investing in apartments.

Chapter 10

APARTMENTS—
ECONOMIES OF
SCALE

- Why would I want all my rental units in one place—an apartment complex—instead of diversified in many different rental houses?
- How do I find apartments for sale?
- How much should I spend on an apartment complex?
- What rents should I charge?
- What vacancy rate is normal in apartments?
- When does it make economic sense to hire a resident manager instead of using a management company?
- Are there any expenses associated with apartments that I might not think about when preparing a budget?
- How can I learn more about this investment vehicle?
- What are the pros and cons of owning apartments rather than single-family homes?
- I do not like the constant tenant turnover encountered with apartments, and my investment budget cannot afford a large complex with professional management. Is there another investment that might work better for me?

Investing in multi-family residential properties—apartments—is hitting the big time. You might want to move up to this after a few years of rental houses or even quadraplexes. Technically, a building with four rental units, a *quadraplex*, is considered multi-family. Conceptually, however, it is usually treated in the same class as single-family residential properties.

Why would I want all my rental units in one place— an apartment complex—instead of diversified in many different rental houses?

The answer to this question depends on your risk tolerance and on how sensitive the apartment complex might be to changes. Admittedly, rental houses all over town may be better than one set of apartments next to a military base that is constantly on the Defense Department closure list each year. That problem is manageable, however, by choosing locations that are not quite so vulnerable.

The apartments will provide important economies of scale on your expenses. Maintenance, management fees, insurance, and major repairs are all cheaper for a thirty-unit apartment complex than for thirty rental houses.

You can sell the entire apartment complex to one buyer if you want, instead of trying to sell many different houses. Apartment owners are not usually area-sensitive. You can find buyers from outside your community and state, which is practically impossible with rental houses.

Satisfied tenants usually recommend your apartments to their friends. That word-of-mouth advertising and referral network happens much less often with single-family residences.

If you want to refinance and pull out some equity for other investments, it is much easier with apartment complexes. Many lenders and many secondary market investment portfolios require that a certain percentage of their loans be in multi-family residential properties. They are considered very safe loans. As a result, it is relatively easy to refinance or place second mortgage loans on apartments.

How do I find apartments for sale?

Sometimes you can find smaller apartment complexes advertised in the local newspaper classifieds, or even in home magazines used by residential real estate agents. Commercial property online listing sites, such as LoopNet at **www.loopnet.com**, are also popular advertising methods.

Local commercial brokers should be knowledgeable regarding properties currently offered for sale. If you are actively looking for something to buy, prepare a short description of what you want, and distribute copies to all the apartment management companies you can find. The description should include your desired number of units, target market if applicable (seniors, students, etc.), and price range. If you intend to retain professional management, say that in your flyer. Why? Because the management company will not be scared to tell you about purchase possibilities in its own portfolio, confident that it will probably not result in a loss of business to them. In addition, I find that management companies know all the gossip around town. If one thinks it can pick up a new account by giving you advice regarding buying a complex managed by another company, it will do so.

How much should I spend on an apartment complex?

This analysis depends on calculating something called the NOI—*Net Operating Income*—and a *cap rate*. See Chapter 18 for more information.

What rents should I charge?

This topic is covered in the chapter on rental rates and security deposits.

What vacancy rate is normal in apartments?

Most sophisticated investors do their financial planning based on a 10% vacancy rate in the apartment complex. Common wisdom says that if your vacancy rate is routinely less than 10%—or your occupancies are greater than 90%, depending on how you want to express it—then your rents are too low.

	Altamont Apartments	Brandywine Apartments
# of units	50	50
Monthly rent each	$1,000	$1,200
Vacancies	0	1 month each for various units, totaling six months rent
Gross potential income	$600,000	$720,000
Income lost to vacancies	$0	$72,000
Vacancy rate	0%	10%
Total income before expenses	$600,000	$648,000

Below is an example to illustrate that point. We will assume that both complexes are comprised of equal-sized and similar quality units.

By charging market rents, the owner of Brandywine Apartments has more vacancies, but also has an extra $48,000 per year to put in his or her pocket.

This is why you should aim for a 90% occupancy rate rather than a 100% occupancy rate.

When does it make economic sense to hire a resident

manager instead of using a management company?

Actually, this is not an either/or situation. You can have a resident manager and a management company without paying a huge amount of money.

A rule of thumb says that a fifty-unit apartment complex will support a resident manager. He or she will need to save you enough money on management company fees, minor repairs, timely rent collections, and lower vacancy rates in order to cover his or her salary and benefits. You will need to factor into your expense the lost revenues from the manager's apartment.

A good on-site manager can result in lower tenant turnover because of the relationship and loyalty felt by the tenants, and because of the manager's ability to quickly respond to problems. A manager with good sales skills can fill vacant units more quickly than off-site management.

Unless you have excellent management skills yourself, I recommend keeping a management company even if you have resident staff at your complex. It is a very unusual manager who can remain motivated and energetic year after year. Employees often become lax about some forms and procedures over time, especially if nothing bad happens as a result. A management company can keep your resident manager happy and fulfilled in his or her job, and focused and consistent regarding all policies and procedures. The resident manager becomes part of a management team.

Of course, if you hire a resident manager but keep your management company, the company should reduce its fees. Many of its former obligations are now being performed by your employee, not its own employee.

As an alternative, many apartment owners ask their management company to place a resident manager at the complex. That person is an employee of the management company. This arrangement insulates the owner from liability for the manager's actions and avoids all employee-related paperwork obligations.

Are there any expenses associated with apartments that I might not think about when preparing a budget?

Owning apartments may expose you to some expenses different than those encountered in single-family housing. When reviewing financial information provided by the seller, ask for the detailed trial balance if available. If not, ask for the check register. Both of these will provide expense details not ordinarily revealed on a profit and loss statement. You want to see exactly what expenses the project has, not just a figure for a general category such as "maintenance." This will give you a good education about the subject. It also gives you an early warning if some expenses have been omitted by the seller in order to make the finances look better.

Depending on the size of the project and how much work you do yourself, you can expect the following additional expenses, besides the normal mortgage payments, taxes, and insurance.

- Electricity for exterior lighting
- Garbage pickup
- Water (Many apartments do not separately meter water for the tenants.)
- Parking lot cleaning
- Tenant move-out expenses, such as lock changes and painting
- Advertising (You will probably need to maintain a listing in a local apartment guide, a phone directory ad, and an online presence.)
- Leasing commissions (Real estate agents may expect a commission, usually one month's rent, for referring tenants to you.)

How can I learn more about this investment vehicle?

Fortunately, apartment owners have their own trade association. It is the *American Apartment Owners Association*. You can contact them at their website, **www.american-apartment-owners-association.org**, or by calling 303-328-2391. I strongly urge you to join this excellent organization. Not only will you learn far more than can be covered in any book, but you will gain many other benefits, including reduced rates for tenant background checks, reviews of specialized management software, forms developed by leading experts, checklists of inspection items with tips on what to look for, and much, much more.

What are the pros and cons of owning apartments rather than single-family homes?

Pros:

- Economies of scale
- One tenant move-out does not result in complete loss of revenues
- Easier to finance
- Easier to sell
- Easier to attract investors and partners
- The market has been stable for many years
- Large enough to support professional management

Cons:

- May be sensitive to demographic changes and population shifts away from that neighborhood
- This is a business, not a supplement to your income. It will require more of your time, even with a management company.

• Constant tenant turnover

I do not like the constant tenant turnover encountered with apartments, and my investment budget cannot afford a large complex with professional management. Is there another investment that might work better for me?

Small office buildings often provide steady, long-term tenants who continue to renew every three or five years. I know of several doctors who have been renting the same space for over twenty years! For more on this subject, read the next chapter, "Office Buildings."

Chapter 11

OFFICE BUILDINGS— LONG-TERM LEASES, BETTER TERMS

- How do I find office buildings for sale?
- What is a fair price to pay for an office building?
- What due diligence is specific to office buildings?
- How do I find a lender for an office building?
- Should I buy an office building with one or two large tenants or many smaller tenants?
- Should I hire a management company?
- How much should I budget for leasing commissions if I own an office building?
- When I am ready to sell my offices, what is the best way to find a buyer?

Many beginning investors prefer small office buildings rather than residential properties. The leases are for longer terms—usually three to five years. Tenants often renew for many years. There are fewer headaches. It is common to back-charge office tenants for all repairs and to make them responsible for their fair share of annual increasing expenses. The same tactic is often difficult or impossible with residential tenants.

How do I find office buildings for sale?

It is very rare to find a "For Sale" sign in the front lawn of an office building. It tends to scare the existing tenants and deter new tenants. You will have to work with a real estate broker, or ask around in the brokerage community regarding properties for sale.

Many more owners would be willing to sell if someone made them an offer. They do no advertising, though, and do not have the property listed with any broker. You will have to find these motivated owners on your own. The best way is to look for properties with high vacancies, but in good buildings with good locations. The high vacancies are probably a management problem. You may find a very motivated owner.

The current tenants might be able to give you contact information for the owner or the management company. If that does not work, the local tax assessor's office can tell you the name of the legal owner and the address where the tax bills are sent.

Bear in mind that a management company is not motivated to pass along information about potential buyers. If the current owner sells the property, the management company might lose an account. If you do not hear back from the management company after several attempts at contacting them, find another route for identifying the owner.

Tip: There are some specialized commercial listing sites on the Internet. One that you can use without being a paid member is LoopNet, at **www.loopnet.com**.

What is a fair price to pay for an office building?

The typical way to evaluate a purchase price for an office building is the *Net Operating Income* (NOI) and *cap rate* method. See Chapter 18 for more information.

The current owner will usually want a sales price based on what the rental income would be if only the property were managed better and had more tenants at higher rates. You will want to buy based on today's dreadful picture, with your upside potential based on improving occupancies and perhaps reducing prices. You are going to agree on a price somewhere between those two. The magic number will depend on your relative motivations and negotiating skills.

What due diligence is specific to office buildings?

This is not comprehensive, but here is a checklist of things to investigate when buying a small office building.

- Read all leases.

- Obtain an owner statement, in writing, that there are no other written or oral agreements.

- Review tenant payment histories over at least the past two years.

- Read all tenant correspondence files, looking especially for recurring complaints.

- Examine maintenance records for at least two years.

- Ask for copies of all maintenance contracts currently in place, and any canceled within the last year.

- Obtain property tax notices for the last three years.

- Review insurance policies and ask for permission to obtain copies of any claims from the insurance company.

- Visit often over the course of several days. Are there any parking or loading issues? Does the inside temperature seem to be well regulated? Does the elevator work? What goes on during the day? Are there any sewer smells in the bathrooms or hallways?

- Visit at night. Do the exterior lights come on? Does the property appear safe?

- Visit when it rains. Where does the water go? Does it exit the property in an appropriate manner, or are there water issues?

- Is the property in compliance with the *Americans With Disabilities Act*? Most bookstores will sell you, or public interest groups will give you, small books and pamphlets with general guidelines. The United States Department of Justice has a good FAQ site at **www.usdoj.gov/crt/ada/ada.html**. It covers employment issues as well as property requirements.

- Enter all office spaces, preferably after hours and with the owner, to perform a physical inspection. You will still need the services of a professional property inspector. Your visit is to evaluate the quality of tenants, and to see if any problems leap out at you so you do not have to spend the money on an inspector. Stained ceiling tiles, for example, are a sure sign of roof or HVAC problems. A high proportion of space heaters is another sign to look for; you will find them underneath desks, even in the summertime. Large numbers of space heaters mean inefficient heating and a high drain on the electrical system with possible overload problems.

- Find out if anything makes that property less competitive than others. Local government lines can meander all over the place. Is your building in some jurisdiction that charges an employment tax for all workers in that building? Is there a rental tax placed on landlords?

How do I find a lender for an office building?

You will probably have to talk to the commercial real estate lender from several financial institutions. Titles and authority vary widely. Be sure to mention the approximate purchase price and the part of town where your office building is located. Ask to be referred to the appropriate people in that lender's company.

Tip: The seller's own lender is also a good candidate. He or she already knows the property and its performance. He or she may be the one most motivated to loan you the money, and the one who can close most quickly.

Should I buy an office building with one or two large tenants or many smaller tenants?

The answer to this question depends on the tenant, your risk tolerance, your financial resources, and what I call the "fooling with it" factor. One or two large tenants can mean nice steady income for many years with a minimum of headaches. The hurt comes when that tenant moves out. The space can remain vacant for a year, sometimes more, until another large tenant can be found. You may have to remodel the space for the new tenant, or to split it into smaller offices for multiple tenants.

> **Tip:** A building with many small offices suffers less impact when one of them moves out. It is also usually easier to replace a smaller tenant.

Office tenants desiring larger space generally expect the landlord to fund a certain amount of what is called *tenant improvements*—TI for short. This could include something as simple as new paint and floor covering to something as large as gutting the space and installing all new walls, doors, lighting, finishes, and cabinetry. The landlord eventually recoups the money from the tenant through higher rents but must front the expenses. That requires a good bit of financial strength with either cash or borrowing power.

Most new investors will not be able to pay the TI up front. The good news is smaller office dwellers do not typically expect this. They are usually happy with new paint and carpet, or even new paint and carpet cleaning. They are generally more flexible regarding office layout. Part of the reason is that they have fewer choices in the marketplace. Large apartment buildings rarely want to fool with small tenants. Most will not rent less than 5,000 square feet to anyone at all. Smaller tenants generally require something in the range of 800 to 3,000 square feet.

Beginning investors should usually focus on office buildings with many smaller tenants. If you can find a single-tenant office building with a national company and nine years left on a ten-year lease, you will probably be facing a bidding war among nationwide investors. It is unlikely that you will be the successful bidder.

Should I hire a management company?

This is a matter of your own time and strengths, and the size of the property. Smaller office buildings may not support the expense of a management company. A residential management company will usually keep tenants in your property without charging any additional fees. A commercial property management company typically charges one fee for pure management and a separate percentage for obtaining new tenants. Make sure you cover that in advance, and have a clear understanding of all fees and expenses. Commercial management companies are also more likely to charge you for copies, long distance calls, mileage, and other such internal expenses.

How much should I budget for leasing commissions if I own an office building?

Leasing commissions vary among markets and brokerage firms. You can still find real estate agents who will charge the equivalent of one or two months' rent as a leasing commission. More typical is a commission based on a percentage of the gross value of the lease. Four percent of the gross lease value seems to be the going rate in many communities.

Example: Suppose Acme Attorneys wishes to rent 3,000 square feet of space in your building for five years. The rental rate you are willing to give them is $23 per square foot per year. Their annual rent will be:

$23 per sq.ft. x 3,000 square feet = $69,000.
Monthly rent is $69,000 ÷ 12 = $5,750
Gross rent over 5 years is $69,000 x 5 = $345,000
4% of $345,000 = $13,800 = commission payable

On a five-year lease, this works out to 2.4 months' rent. Similar calculations for a three-year lease work out to 1.44 months' rent as a leasing commission.

Before making a snap decision to pay a percentage commission or a certain number of months' rent, do the math to see which method works out better for you.

When I am ready to sell my offices, what is the best way to find a buyer?

Your three best prospects for a buyer are:

- existing tenants who would prefer to own rather than rent;
- other owner-clients of your current property management firm, if you have one. It is an easy decision for clients to buy more properties if they are satisfied with their property managers; and,
- landlords who own nearby, similar properties. Find them by driving around and doing research in the real estate records or by asking tenants who owns their buildings.

If these obvious sources of buyers do not work, think about hiring a real estate broker or doing some intensive advertising and marketing. It is usually harder to find a buyer for a commercial property than for a home. The potential buyers are spread over a wider geographic area and take longer to make decisions. A broker will usually ask for a one-year listing agreement and a higher commission because of that.

Many office building investors choose a strategy of buying properties, improving occupancies and rental rates, and then selling the building for a large profit. Tenant selection can be an important part of that strategy. Try to find at least one good local tenant who has the possibility of buying your building in the future. If it does well at that location, he or she might want to be a property owner rather than a tenant in a few years. The other tenants in the building could remain in place, providing valuable rental income, until the tenant-owner needs to expand and take over additional space. Law firm tenants are always good prospects for this strategy, which is called *grow your own buyer.*

Chapter 12

CONVENIENCE STORES—FAST DEPRECIATION WRITE-OFFS

- How can I find convenience stores for sale?
- How much should I pay for a convenience store?
- What due diligence will I need for a convenience store?
- What is the biggest risk encountered with convenience stores?
- What is the biggest upside potential for investment in convenience stores?
- I like the retail portion of convenience stores, but those underground gas tanks worry me. What other investment options might be available?

Convenience stores are very desirable investments because of the fast tax write-offs. A residential property can be depreciated over 27.5 years. A commercial property must be depreciated over 39 years. A convenience store, however, can be written off over a very short 15-year time period, if you meet other IRS requirements. Because of these tax-sheltering benefits, they often bring higher asking prices than you might otherwise expect.

How can I find convenience stores for sale?

As always, check out the local real estate brokers, advertising places, and websites for commercial properties. In addition, look for properties with signs of distress, which might have motivated owners to sell. Depending on your local laws and prevailing opinions, a convenience store that does not sell alcoholic beverages may have some sort of problem obtaining a license. Pumps that seem to be frequently out of order or a number of lights that do not work at night indicate an owner who cannot afford a maintenance contract or repair bills. Sparsely-filled shelves mean the owner's vendor cut off the credit, and will only deliver items *cash on delivery* (COD).

Develop a relationship with the independent oil and gas providers, because they will know all the gossip all over town. If anyone wants to sell, his or her gas supplier will know it first.

> **Tip:** You may also be able to find listings on commercial websites such as LoopNet, at **www.loopnet.com**, or on the website for the National Association of Convenience Stores, **www.nacsonline.com**.

How much should I pay for a convenience store?

Convenience stores sold as operating businesses are typically priced as a multiple of *Earnings Before Interest, Taxes, Depreciation, and Amortization* (EBITDA). Basically, that means a certain multiple of the annual cash flows, such as three times annual cash flow up to around seven times annual cash flow. The value of the underlying real estate and the condition of the building, tanks, and pumps does not add or subtract from that number, it simply determines if the sales price is closer to 3 x EBITDA or 7 x EBITDA.

Convenience stores sold strictly as real estate, with a tenant in place who owns and operates the actual store, are sold based on the NOI and cap rate evaluation method. See Chapter 18 for more information.

What due diligence will I need for a convenience store?

I am assuming that you will buy a convenience store as a real estate investment, not as an operating business. In other words, you will have a tenant who will run the business. Re-read the chapter devoted to due diligence. Some of the items peculiar to other types of properties are also relevant here. They are reprinted below. Additionally, you will need to investigate the following.

- Anything and everything having to do with the underground tanks. A specific state agency in every state is devoted to this critical area. The seller can tell you how to get in touch with it. It will tell you if there is any history of spills or non-compliance. You will also need a specialists' *property inspection report*. It should be someone with extensive experience in gas station properties. Even if you did not cause the spill, even if it occurred before you purchased the property, you could be liable for all cleanup expenses.

- Copies of all environmental insurance policies, proof they have not been canceled for nonpayment or other reasons, and the cost of those policies.

- The local highway or streets/roads department can tell you if there are any plans to change nearby roads. A change in traffic patterns can be deadly for a convenience store. Simply taking away a traffic light or widening some lanes can make entering and exiting the property more difficult and affect sales. If your tenant goes out of business, you might not be able to find another one.

- Read the agreement between the convenience store owner and its *jobber*—gas supplier. The jobber may have early warnings in place for the possibility of default, or may have remedies that affect your cash flow.

- Read all leases, especially those for fast-food companies that operate at the site.

What is the biggest risk encountered with convenience stores?

The risk is in the ground—the gas tanks. Leaking underground storage tanks (LUSTs) can cause massive cleanup expenses, not just for the gas station operator, but also for the owner of the property. Insurance is very expensive and will need to be maintained by the property owner if the operator goes out of business.

Related to that risk is the possibility of expensive new government requirements regarding the tanks or the pumps. Not too long ago, all underground tanks in the country had to be replaced with newer, double-walled tanks that minimized the risk of leaks. Property owners had a certain time limit to complete the replacement or to fill in the old tanks with concrete and cease operations. Something similar could happen in the future.

What is the biggest upside potential for investment in convenience stores?

Aside from the rapid tax write-offs, I think the most exciting thing about investing in convenience stores is the possibility of very large resale profits in the near future. Yes, the smaller operators are facing tremendous pressure from the national and regional chains and the efficiencies they enjoy because of their size. But, the industry is still largely fragmented into smaller owners and operators. The big players are buying up the smaller ones, engaged in something called *industry consolidation*. Every time an industry undergoes consolidation, sellers with good locations can command premium prices because of their strategic value.

I like the retail portion of convenience stores, but those underground gas tanks worry me. What other investment options might be available?

You might be better suited for investments with retail, restaurant, or fast-food tenants. Read the next chapter, "Retail and Dining," for more information.

Chapter 13

RETAIL AND DINING— GOING AFTER THE NATIONAL TENANTS

- How do I find retail properties for sale?
- What if I cannot find any good retail properties in my community? Can I still invest?
- How can I find NNN properties for sale?
- How much should I pay for a NNN lease property?
- What happens at the end of the lease term if a NNN tenant moves out?
- I do not want to invest in far-off cities, but right where I live. What are some things I should consider regarding whether a location is a good investment?
- What retail and dining trends might have an impact on the success of any tenant I have?
- Is there anything special I should know about retail and dining leases?
- I would like to have some large national companies as tenants, but I cannot afford to build the specialized buildings most of them seem to need. Is there another way to capture that market?

According to the U.S. Department of Agriculture, Americans spend about half their food dollars eating out, rather than buying groceries to prepare at home. This percentage has been increasing steadily for over thirty years, and is expected to rise even more in the future. The same agency reports that we spend about 10% of our disposable income on food in general. That means 5% of our disposable income goes into the bank accounts of restaurants and fast-food establishments. For you, as a potential landlord for such businesses, this is terrific news.

Retail sales are relatively soft as of the writing of this book. In addition, online purchases are increasing dramatically, as Internet shopping becomes an easy and safe way to buy things. Both of those trends are eating into the investor/landlord's profits because of the fierce competition among property owners to attract strong retail tenants. Despite that, investing in retail properties can be very profitable, if you are sensitive to certain key issues described in this chapter.

How do I find retail properties for sale?

You will almost always have to work through a broker to obtain that information. Consumer confidence is such an important part of retail sales that no one wants to upset it with rumors that the actual real estate is for sale. Most people draw no distinction between property for sale and the business located on the property being for sale. Those that do recognize the difference assume the landlord is selling because he or she knows, ahead of everyone else, that the tenant is in financial trouble.

What if I cannot find any good retail properties in my community? Can I still invest?

Fortunately for you, one of the strongest investment trends in recent years is in something called *triple-net leases*, usually seen written as NNN leases. Many nationwide brokerage firms, such as Marcus & Millichap (**www.marcusmillichap.com**), list these investment opportunities in locations as diverse as San Francisco, California, and Eufala, Alabama.

This is how NNN leases work. Typically, a developer will buy a piece of land. Using his or her contacts, the developer will find a company such as Walgreens, Subway, or Starbucks that wishes to be at that location. The developer will sign a long-term lease, usually twenty years with several five-year renewals at the option of the tenant. Next, the developer builds a building according to the tenant's specifications exactly. The tenant takes occupancy and pays rent every month, plus takes care of all maintenance, upkeep, repairs, renovations, taxes, and insurance. The developer/landlord does absolutely nothing except deposit the rent check every month.

The developer then sells the property as a category of investment called a NNN lease. That indicates to any purchaser that a long-term, financially strong tenant is in place and the landlord has absolutely no financial or management responsibilities. Investors do the equivalent of buying a long-term certificate of deposit, except in real estate. The investor's confidence is in the tenant. If you trust Walgreens and think it will pay its bills for the next twenty years, you really do not care if it is your tenant in your hometown or in a semirural area one thousand miles away.

How can I find NNN properties for sale?

The Marcus & Millichap website previously mentioned requires registration before you can view properties, but there is no charge. To search on the Internet for other brokers, search for "NNN lease investments." You will find more sites than you will have time to sift through.

How much should I pay for a NNN lease property?

Your purchase price will depend on something called a *discounted cash flow analysis*. This sounds complicated, but it is really pretty easy. Read Chapter 18 for an explanation of this calculation.

What happens at the end of the lease term if a NNN tenant moves out?

You still own the real estate. You can hire a broker and sell or rent it to someone else. Or, if you received all the value you wanted from the property, are satisfied with your returns, and do not want to think about it anymore, just fail to pay the real estate taxes the next time they are due. Someone in that community will buy the property for the tax bill. I do not recommend that route; I am just throwing it out there as the absolute worst that can happen. If you think about what a pain it might be to fool with that empty real estate, you gain a good insight into why national companies would often rather rent than own.

I do not want to invest in far-off cities, but right where I live. What are some things I should consider regarding whether a location is a good investment?

The retail and dining industries are where that old real estate mantra, "location, location, location" becomes especially important. The very best locations will always attract the strongest tenants willing to pay the highest prices. Below are some location considerations that might be important, depending on the type of tenant you want to attract.

- High local traffic counts are important. Large numbers of high-speed cars commuting but never stopping will not help you very much. Call your local highway department or department of transportation and ask how you can find traffic counts. They are usually online.

- Rooftops are important for neighborhood businesses. How many households are in the area? Is it growing, stable, or going into decline?

- Most retail and dining establishments do better on the going-home side of the road than the going-to-work side of the road. Exceptions are coffee- and breakfast-related businesses, which naturally want the morning traffic.

- When choosing among corners, the one just past the traffic light is better. A business right before a busy traffic light will have exit problems. Consumers trying to pull out onto the street will often be blocked by cars waiting at the red light.

- Placement of *curb cuts* (how people on your side of the road enter the property), *median cuts* (how people traveling in the other direction enter your property), and the existence of so-called *suicide lanes* (turn lanes) can dramatically affect business success or failure.

- For retail and dining, you do not want to be the only show in town. In other words, locations with a lot of other retail and dining options do not mean you will have a lot of competition. It means that many people will drive to that general area for shopping or dining, and then make a decision about which particular place to go. All tenants will do well.

What retail and dining trends might have an impact on the success of any tenant I have?

One of the more noticeable trends is to shop or dine for entertainment. It seems that consumers require more and more stimulation in their lives. Businesses that deliver those experiences will do better than those that deliver only goods or food. Think about all the television advertising you see. Everyone is having fun, things are exciting, it is an adventure to shop or take your meals with the advertised businesses. Look for similar traits in the tenants for any such real estate investment.

Trends can change pretty quickly. This is an area where you should invest in specialty magazines or newsletters. You can go to the *New York Times*–owned website **www.about.com** and search on "retail industry" for a wealth of resources.

Is there anything special I should know about retail and dining leases?

There are always many different ways to structure a lease. It is very common in these industries to have a *base rent*, plus a percentage of the gross sales at that location. When offered the option of a high gross sales percentage and a low base rent, weigh the consequences if the tenant decides to close shop. Even 95% of no sales is still nothing, so you might be stuck with a very small monthly rent and nothing more.

What is worse, the tenant might not allow you to sublease the space to someone else or cancel its lease. What if you had a Wal-Mart as a tenant, but it closed its store at your location and moved down the street three blocks to something larger? Wal-Mart might be willing to pay you a paltry base rent each month in order to prevent you from leasing to Target or Sears. Do not think these shenanigans happen only with the giants—much smaller tenants with good lawyers or a willingness to learn tricks from the big guys also employ these tactics.

You should also be aware of something called the *going dark clause*. Usually, it prohibits the tenant from closing its doors, turning out the lights, and "going dark" but continuing to pay the rent each month. Oftentimes, the clause will specify how many days and hours a business must operate, the number of staff that must be on hand, and even that the store must stock merchandise. It is an important clause in shopping centers, which often depend on the presence of particular large tenants to attract business for the other tenants, called *satellites* or *juniors*. You can use a variant of that clause by allowing yourself the right to cancel the lease and sublease to anyone else if the tenant does not maintain a certain minimum sales level, but this must be in your lease.

I would like to have some large national companies as tenants, but I cannot afford to build the specialized buildings most of them seem to need. Is there another way to capture that market?

You can often join forces with a developer who has the borrowing strength to build the improvements and the contacts to secure national tenants. The preferred method for such an arrangement is something called the *ground lease*. It is not a partnership, but a straight lease. Ground leases are covered in the next chapter.

Chapter 14

RAW LAND AND GROUND LEASES— RENTING DIRT

- Why would anyone rent dirt instead of buying?
- I see "For Lease" signs on raw land all over my community. Does this mean it is a very popular investment strategy in this area?
- I have a lot of experience leasing other properties. Can I negotiate my own ground leases?
- Can you give an example of a dangerous clause in a ground lease?
- What due diligence is specific to buying land for ground leases?
- What should I spend for land if I plan to ground lease it?
- How much should I charge for ground rent?
- Ground leases are usually long-term leases. Should I increase the rent periodically?
- I feel like Gerald O'Hara in *Gone With the Wind*. I want to invest in land, and more land. My friends think I am crazy. What can I tell them?
- How can I determine where the "path of progress" is going?

Many investors buy *raw land* and then rent that land to someone else who builds an improvement on it. This is called *ground leasing*. For example, you might own a piece of land at a very popular intersection. It is not going to do anything except grow in value. You would like some income from it, but you do not want to sell. Drug stores, fast-food chains, and any number of other companies will rent your land for twenty years, pay to build their own building, and in the end you have the land and the building.

Developers are also willing to execute ground leases. They would prefer to buy the real estate, but they may not be able to obtain prime land in good locations. Developers do not make any money unless they develop—they are often forced to ground lease in order to stay in business.

Why would anyone rent dirt instead of buying?

Some have no choice. They want the best location in town, right now, but no one has anything for sale. If that company is going to be in business in that marketplace, it is forced to ground lease. Others choose this vehicle because they do not want any ownership headaches when they elect to abandon a site. If, after twenty years, the marketplace has changed, they can simply pack up and leave. There is no property to maintain on the books, no insurance to keep up, no maintenance, and no real estate broker to pay.

I see "For Lease" signs on raw land all over my community. Does this mean it is a very popular investment strategy in this area?

In some markets, ground leasing is very popular with property owners, even if it is not popular with potential tenants. Every other piece of land has a "For Lease" sign on it. As a practical matter, the ground lease marketplace is not that large. Before leaping into it, pay attention to the signs around town. Are they in places you consider good locations? Are the asking rents reasonable, in your opinion? How long do the signs stay up? If the signs have been up so long that the letters have faded in the sun, it might not be such a good market or location.

I have a lot of experience leasing other properties. Can I negotiate my own ground leases?

Ground lease documents are usually written by high-powered lawyers who charge $500 per hour and work on the 40th floor of office towers in big cities. This is not an area in which you can read a lease yourself and understand what you are signing. Your real estate broker, if you have one, will not be able to advise you. Pay the money for an expert attorney to review the lease. You might want to hold down legal fees by doing your own negotiating and keeping your lawyer in the background for consultations.

> **Tip:** I never tell anyone the name of my lawyer unless I need that name for credibility. The reason is because once someone thinks they have reached a roadblock with me, they always call my lawyer. They try to enlist *my* lawyer's help for *their* cause. It never works, but I still receive a bill for the time my lawyer spent talking to the other side, reviewing correspondence the prospective tenant sent to me but copied my lawyer on, and other such nonsense. I want to make sure I am the only one running my attorney's meter.

Can you give an example of a dangerous clause in a ground lease?

It is common for ground leases to have a subordination clause buried somewhere after the point you go cross-eyed reading dozens of pages of fine print. If you sign, you are agreeing to subordinate to the tenant's construction lender or possibly even any other lender. That means that the lender will take a mortgage on the *leasehold interest* (the only thing your tenant "owns") and on *your* property. If the ground tenant defaults on its mortgage, you lose your land also. Without the subordination clause, the lender who forecloses on the building and the leasehold interest must keep paying you the ground rent every month. If they do not, you can declare the lease in default and then you will own everything free and clear—the dirt, the building, and all other improvements.

What due diligence is specific to buying land for ground leases?

By and large, you want to make sure of the following.

- The property is zoned properly for all anticipated uses. Never, never, never rely on a public official telling you that "rezoning will be a slam dunk." If the land is not currently zoned for use by the tenants you have in mind, condition closing on being able to obtain that rezoning or zoning variance.

- The land is buildable, considering all setback and other requirements. A lot that is 50 feet wide by 50 feet deep, but with local laws prohibiting any buildings within 30 feet of the property line, is virtually un-buildable. It is not just the physical building you must consider, but also required drive lanes, turn-arounds, and parking.

- The soil is compacted enough to support structures without expensive additional work. An engineer can answer those questions for you.

- There is no history of any potential hazardous waste discharge. Many investors buy raw land when they come into a cash windfall. As a result, they do not need any financing, so there is no lender around to require a *Phase I Environmental Report*— the report that alerts you to the possibility of hazardous waste on the property. This is especially a problem with raw land because you usually think it is pristine—pure and clean—but you could be wrong.

- Where are the utilities? If you do not have nearby utilities, especially storm and sanitary sewers, it will be very expensive for someone to build on the property, or it could be completely impossible. You might not be allowed to tap into existing sewer lines.

- Is the land in the city limits or not? Building requirements can be completely different inside the city limits than outside. This will affect the cost of construction.

- It is a little thing, but one often overlooked by new investors. What side of the road is the property on? Where is most of the nearby development? Most fast-food and retail chains like to be on the "going home" side of the road. If you are on the "going to work" side of the road, your property will take much longer to market.

What should I spend for land if I plan to ground lease it?

Refer to Chapter 18. You will use the discounted cash flow analysis method to calculate an offering price. You can do that if you already have in mind a particular tenant and know how much ground rent that tenant is willing to pay. If you are buying land as a speculative venture, then read the following questions regarding raw land.

How much should I charge for ground rent?

Start with the value of the land. How much would it cost you to buy that land today? Disregard what you actually paid for it. Next, ask yourself how much you would want it to earn each year if the land were a bank account. Would you want a 6% return on your money, or maybe 10%? Of course, we would all like to earn 200% on our investments every year, but that is not possible. Be realistic. The marketplace will usually pay something between 4% and 10%.

Once you establish your desired return, talk to brokers and potential tenants. See if your rental rate is considered reasonable. If so, that is the amount you should charge.

Ground leases are usually long-term leases. Should I increase the rent periodically?

Yes, your ground lease should provide for rent increases at least every five years. How much depends on which one of three methods you choose.

1. Proportionate increase based on the increased value of the real estate. This will require appraisal expenses and can lead to disputes among competing appraisers (yours and the tenant's) and a lawsuit unless you have a mediation clause.

2. Predetermined increases, which might result in the tenant paying above-market rates (bad for them, good for you) in the future, or below-market rates (good for them, bad for you.)

3. A percentage of gross sales at the location. Please re-read the discussion of percentage rent in the chapter "Retail and Dining," because you will need to be concerned about some of the same issues.

I strongly recommend using an experienced ground lease broker to negotiate these transactions. As a fallback, read everything you can about the subject. I can recommend *Commercial Ground Leases* by Jerome D. Whalen. It is expensive—a little over $200—but far cheaper than a lawyer spending the time to give you the same general education. I am not saying you should dispense with the lawyer. I am saying that you should use his or her time wisely by being a more knowledgeable investor and asking the right questions. You can preview the book, to see if it is worth the money to you, by doing a Google book search. Your local library might also have a copy, especially a nearby business college library.

I feel like Gerald O'Hara in *Gone With the Wind*. I want to invest in land, and more land. My friends think I am crazy. What can I tell them?

There are many excellent reasons to invest in raw land. Below are a few answers you can give your friends.

- You can buy well-positioned land in the path of progress very cheaply. When the area matures, you may be able to sell the land for ten or twenty times what you paid for it. Think about this— people buy such land by the acre, but they sell it by the square foot. There are 43,560 square feet in an acre. A seemingly outrageous purchase price of $50,000 per acre in 1998, might become $10 per foot—$435,600 per acre—or more in 2008. Corners are especially valuable.

- Undeveloped land can often be rented to others until it has matured. Potential tenants include agricultural uses for pasturage, mobile home sales lots, and utility company vehicle parking.

- If it is covered in harvestable trees, the timber itself can provide valuable income. The federal government, and many state governments, subsidize planting pine seedlings on land.

How can I determine where the "path of progress" is going?

That is the important question when investing in raw land. Find out where new schools will be built. Local governments make those decisions several years in advance. They usually have more money to spend on consultants and specialists than you do. You can ride their coattails. Besides, building new schools becomes a self-fulfilling prophecy for growth. The schools go where they anticipate growth. People move where the new schools are. Retail businesses follow the rooftops.

Growth will proceed first along the major thoroughfares and arteries. As long as people can travel these routes to work in a reasonable amount of time each morning, new construction will continue outward. When the drive-time becomes intolerable according to local expectations, developers will begin expanding with more depth, but closer to important interchanges or to work.

Chapter 15

WORKING WITH AGENTS—BUYING OR SELLING: FIND THE BEST

- Is a real estate agent the same as a REALTOR®?
- Every real estate agent I know has a lot of initials after his or her name. What do all those initials mean?
- What exactly does a real estate agent do?
- What does a discount broker do?
- Do I really need a real estate agent?
- Do real estate agents specialize?
- How do I find the best agent?
- Will my agent keep my information and plans confidential?
- What things should my agent and I agree on?
- What is a typical real estate commission?
- What is the typical term of a listing contract?
- What is the typical term of a buyer-agency agreement?
- Are there different types of agency agreements?
- I would prefer to try things on my own, without any agent. Can I do that?

Working with a real estate agent can be the most productive or the most wasteful activity of your investing career. Choosing the right agent, and knowing exactly how to best work with that person, can make all the difference.

Is a real estate agent the same as a REALTOR®?

Although you will often see references to "realtors," that format is incorrect. A REALTOR® is a member of the National Association of REALTOR® (NAR), the trade association for real estate professionals. One is not required to belong to NAR to sell real estate. The name varies among states, but a real estate agent, broker, licensee, or salesperson is someone who has been licensed by the state and is allowed to represent others in real estate transactions. They might or might not also be a REALTOR®.

A REALTOR® would have you believe that he or she enjoys superior education, motivation, enthusiasm, knowledge, and ethical standards over a nonmember. I think that a very high percentage of members can honestly claim these attributes because of their willingness to commit to the organization and its ideals. Certainly they have access to an incredible array of training, resources, tools, and networking opportunities. When deciding who to hire, you will have to make your own decisions regarding whether a REALTOR® has taken advantage of those opportunities or not and whether a nonmember has equal or superior capabilities even though he or she chose not to join a trade association.

Every real estate agent I know has a lot of initials after his or her name. What do all those initials mean?

There is a wide variety of designations offered by many different real estate–related organizations. There is no consistency among them regarding educational or testing requirements to obtain the designation, nor continuing education requirements to keep them. Bear in mind that some people collect designations like others collect pet rocks. For other people, the education leading up to being granted those initials is a meaningful and important part of their careers and adds value to the services they give their clients and customers.

With that disclaimer, here are a few of the more common designations. Remember, designations that seem similar might not be differing levels of expertise, but simply competing organizations that grant designations. If you do not see one here, look on the website of RealtyU® at **www.coursedates.com/designations.htm** for the list it attempts to keep completely up to date.

- ASR—Accredited Seller Representative
- ABR—Accredited Buyer Representative
- AHWD—At Home With Diversity
- ALHS—Accredited Luxury Home Specialist
- CBR—Certified Buyer Representative
- CEBA—Certified Exclusive Buyers Agent
- CFS—Certified Financial Specialist
- GRI—Graduate REALTOR® Institute
- SRES—Seniors Real Estate Specialist
- CCIM—Certified Commercial Investment Member
- SIOR—Society of Office and Industrial REALTORS®

What exactly does a real estate agent do?

The responsibilities of real estate agents can vary widely from state to state, and also depend on the particular contractual arrangements allowed in each state. There are differences depending on whether you are the client or a customer. Agents owe more to their clients than to their customers.

Whether you are a client or customer depends on state variations in agency law, real estate licensing law, and your own contract or lack thereof. Be sure to ask about these specific issues before entering into a relationship and divulging any confidential information.

As a general rule, a real estate agent is like any other professional. Real estate agents are able to help you work more efficiently because of their superior access to specialized training and information, his or her insider status in the marketplace, their willingness to do the time-consuming chores, and their negotiation skills. However, you cannot just check out and let your agent do everything. You are a team, and every team must have a clear understanding regarding goals, who will do what to reach the goals, how they will do it, and when the parties will get together to discuss progress.

What does a discount broker do?

Discount real estate brokers unbundle the features previously listed. The most common type of *discount broker* will sell you some of his or her insider status in the marketplace by listing your property on the local Multiple Listing Service (MLS) or a nationwide commercial website such as LoopNet. You usually either pay a flat fee for this service, or you pay a reduced commission.

Other services, such as advice, marketing materials, checklists, forms, and screening interested parties might be available for a separate fee. Generally speaking, the discount broker will not show your property to anyone or negotiate on your behalf. Before entering into any relationship with a discount broker, you should have a clear agreement regarding what services are—and what services are not—included. The agent should provide this to you in writing, along with an explanation of how he or she will be compensated.

Do I really need a real estate agent?

This is going to depend on your experience and your personality. Beginning investors with any qualms at all about their knowledge of the market should usually employ an agent. I once represented a buyer who was looking for land on which to build a commercial stable. She called me one day, raving about something she had found. It was perfect, according to her. I drove up to investigate and found a beautiful piece of land, ideal for the high-end clientele she was seeking. Unfortunately, the farm next door raised swine. My client did not notice because the wind was blowing from the other direction that day. Because of my prior real estate experience, I was sensitive to these types of issues regarding neighbors and knew to investigate.

Eventually, you will reach the point at which you will have equal or superior knowledge regarding your type of investments. Even when that day comes, though, you still might choose to employ a real estate agent for his or her contacts, legwork, assistance, and distance.

Distance is sometimes important when negotiating. By *distance*, I mean the ability of an agent to say, "I think that is a good counteroffer and can recommend it, but my client is another matter. I will have to get back to you." In face-to-face negotiations between parties, you sometimes find yourself agreeing to things and then later changing your mind when you have time to think more carefully about them. Having an agent avoids this problem.

Remember that the real estate agent does this for a living. If you are buying, the agent will not show you For Sale By Owner (FSBO) properties because the owner of a FSBO property will usually not pay a commission to the agent. This is unfortunate because many agents probably know about many bargains in the FSBO market. You might want to discuss your willingness to pay a 3% or so commission to your agent if he or she finds a FSBO that you decide to purchase, if the seller will not pay a commission. Three percent is usually about what your real estate agent would make if you bought property listed by another agent.

Do real estate agents specialize?

Many agents specialize if their market will allow them to earn a living in that specialty. A small town will not support an agent who specializes in selling retail properties, for example. Retail properties in small towns just do not change hands often enough for a real estate agent to make a living solely off those commissions.

Generally speaking, these are the different types of specialties. Many agents further specialize by location and price range.

- Owner-occupied residential
- Condominiums
- Resort and vacation properties
- Single-family residential rental properties
- Multi-family residential rental properties
- Commercial, which might be further broken down by retail, office, fast-food, and convenience stores
- Hospitality properties such as hotels and motels
- Specialty, such as self-storage, entertainment, and nursing homes
- Industrial and warehouse
- Farmland
- Hunting and fishing land
- Raw land for development of all types

It is relatively common for persons who identify themselves as residential real estate agents to also take a few listings on other types of properties.

How do I find the best agent?

To find the best agent, start by talking to people who invest in the same types of properties as you currently have or desire to buy. Lenders in that field will also be knowledgeable. Do any agents provide seminars on your topic? What do agents advertise about themselves?

When you have about a dozen names of agents, call each of them. Ask some initial screening questions about their experience in your specialty interest and whether they usually represent buyers or sellers. Have a few market-related questions ready even though you already know the answers. You want to test the agent to see if he or she also knows the answer. No fair asking anything tricky or obscure—the goal here is to hire a good agent, not to flunk some student you think is obnoxious.

When you have the field narrowed down to three people, schedule in-person interviews. You want to see if your personalities are compatible. Does the agent listen to you and give appropriate responses, or does he or she seem intent on selling him- or herself and obtaining a contract? Is he or she confident, dressed in a manner appropriate to his or her specialty, and organized? Is he or she clear and straightforward regarding services and fees? Ask what makes him or her better than the competition. Does he or she immediately give you solid reasons, fumble for an answer, or resort to trashing his or her competitors? Does he or she interact in a professional manner, or does he or she seem flippant, vulgar, or too personal? By the end of the interviews, you should be in a position to hire an agent.

Will my agent keep my information and plans confidential?

Your agent is obligated to keep all your information and plans confidential. There are three problems with this in real life.

1. Buyers often work with a real estate agent who is really the subagent of the seller. In other words, the listing agent represents the seller, but the agent you are working with—even if he or she from a different company—also represents the seller. In that situation, your information will not be kept confidential. In fact, the agent will be obligated to reveal everything to his or her actual client—the seller. If you want something kept confidential, make sure you have something in writing stating that you are the client and the agent represents you. This is a subtle point that some agents do not understand and many have difficulty explaining to consumers.

2. Unfortunately, a few agents misunderstand their responsibilities regarding confidentiality, or they simply do not care or are careless. For example, I once bought a piece of property that had been listed for $219,000, but I was prepared to offer $185,000. The seller's agent, desperate to make a sale before her listing expired, told me that the seller was on the verge of bankruptcy and would be grateful to get $155,000 for the property. That is what I offered and that is what I paid for the piece of property. The agent should never have shared that information with me.

3. Some agents will keep absolutely secret all your financial circumstances but think it is okay to blab your investment plans to every other agent in town. The first time you have a great, creative idea and someone beats you to it, you will know why this is so important. Do not take chances. Stress to the agent that your specific plans and identity should be kept confidential, although the agent can ask others if they have listings on the general type of property you are seeking.

What things should my agent and I agree on?

Generally speaking, you should have a clear agreement on goals, responsibilities, communications, and payment. Of the four, communication failures cause the most lawsuits, and payment issues cause the most surprises.

Your agent cannot work well for you if he or she does not have a clear idea of your goals.

Require the agent to provide you with a general marketing plan *before* you sign the contract with him or her. If the agent's entire plan consists of checking Multiple Listing Service (MLS) for potential purchases, or putting a yard sign out to sell your property, you should know that in advance. You cannot possibly know if your agent is doing a good job if you do not know what his or her job is.

You should also agree on how often the agent will supply you with progress reports and what information should be in those reports. Do you want a list of all contacts with a synopsis of the content, or do you want only the high points?

Have a specific discussion and agreement regarding turnaround time to return phone calls and emails.

Proper communication also means having a clear understanding of what the agent will do for you, what he or she will not do, and his or her responsibilities regarding warning you about property defects, overpricing, or other such dangers. You must also completely understand who the agent represents—you or the seller. Ask as many questions as you need to satisfy yourself on these issues.

What is a typical real estate commission?

For single-family residential properties, the typical listing commission is usually from 6% to 7%. In a seller's market, that can go much lower. Commercial agents generally charge a higher rate, up to around 10%.

That rate will slide downward as the price goes up. You usually will not see a 10% commission on a $10,000,000 property.

Most contracts provide that the listing agent's commission is fully earned at the point he or she provides a buyer who is ready, willing, and able to purchase at price and terms acceptable to the seller. In other words, if the agent brings a full price offer with no contingencies, and the seller decides to reject it and ask for more, the seller probably owes the commission even if there is never another offer and no sale. In addition, if the seller accepts an offer, but then refuses to go through with closing, or cannot complete closing because of title problems, he or she will still owe the agent a full commission.

Buyers' agents/brokers, who represent buyers and go out to find properties for them, typically charge from 4% up to around 10% if they find a seller who will not pay a commission.

What is the typical term of a listing contract?

Most residential listing contracts are for six months, although they may be as short as four months in hot markets. Most commercial property listing contracts are for a minimum of one year and may be as long as eighteen months. The longer time period is because of the smaller pool of potential buyers and the frequent need to expose the property to a nationwide audience. Also, it takes longer to make buying decisions at the corporate level than the household level. For those reasons, it usually takes longer to sell a commercial property.

Many listing contracts have something called an *override* clause. It entitles the agent to his or her commission if the property sells to someone who learned about the property from the agent but purchases it within some time period after the listing expired. That time period is usually six months. The intent is to protect the agent in case he or she finds a buyer within the last few months or weeks of the listing period, but closing does not take place until afterward.

It is also to protect agents from dishonest sellers who wait until the expiration of the listing agreement and then contact the potential buyer themselves.

If your property is unsold at the end of the listing period, you should ask for a list of the people the agent considers covered by the override clause. You can give that list of names to any new agent you hire, and require that a sale to those buyers will not result in a commission being due to your new agent also. Otherwise, you could find yourself legally obligated to pay two full commissions to two different agents.

What is the typical term of a buyer-agency agreement?

These agreements are much more a matter of negotiation than custom. You and the agent must set a reasonable time limit that takes into consideration the relative difficulty of finding a property that is right for you. If you want a one-story ranch-style house with three bedrooms and two bathrooms in a good school district, selling for the average selling price in that area, I would think that a two-month contract would be plenty of time. Finding a mansion in perfect condition for 25% of the appraised value might take a little longer.

Are there different types of agency agreements?

There are several types of agency agreements, usually with differences about the degree of exclusivity.

- The *Exclusive Right to Sell Agency Agreement* means the agent earns a full commission no matter who sells the property. Even if the agent has done absolutely nothing and you sell the property to your mother, you will be obligated to pay the commission.

- The *Exclusive Right to List Agency Agreement* means the agent is the only agent entitled to list the property and find buyers through marketing efforts. If you find a buyer without any assistance from the agent, you do not pay a commission. Disputes arise over questions regarding whose efforts turned up the buyer. Did your coworker learn about the property from you or from the half-page ad the agent placed in the Sunday paper?

- An *Open Listing* is really an offer you make to all real estate agents. You offer to pay them a certain commission if they bring you a buyer and you sell to that person. The commission is generally a little bit higher than the split they would receive with a typical listing agreement. Any agent can accept your offer simply by bringing you such a buyer.

- An *Exclusive Buyer's Agency Agreement* obligates you to pay your agent a commission even if you find property through your own efforts and then buy it. The thinking is that the agent has educated you immensely through the process of searching for properties. He or she should not do that for free.

- A *Non-Exclusive Buyer's Agency Agreement* prevents you from working with other real estate agents to purchase property. If you find something on your own, though, you do not pay a commission.

Note: Transaction brokers have different names in different states. They usually engage in no marketing or sales efforts, but simply assist the parties with advice regarding deal points that should be negotiated, inspections and such prior to sale, and all the paperwork and other things that must come together for closing to take place.

I would prefer to try things on my own, without any agent. Can I do that?

Of course you can! The next chapter tells you how to do it with the least amount of pain. Be aware, however, that real estate agents are part of a fairly close community. Many of them will tell each other non-confidential information they would never share with you as an outsider. You might have to work a little harder by yourself, but at least you can be sure you will not become discouraged and give up. Often, if a real estate agent cannot obtain quick results for someone, he or she moves on to other clients and customers.

Chapter 16

Working without an Agent—Advice for Buyers

- What are the pros and cons of buying property without a real estate agent?
- Can I find Multiple Listing Service (MLS) properties if I do not have an agent?
- What are other ways to find real estate for sale?
- Will sellers take me seriously if I do not have an agent?
- Will a seller reduce his or her price if I don't have an agent representing me?
- How do I make an offer?
- Why do I want to require that the contract is assignable?
- Is earnest money required?
- How much earnest money should I offer?
- What should I put in the seller financing part of the offer?
- What is due diligence?
- I have a due diligence clause. Why do I also need a contingencies clause?
- What are encumbrances?
- The seller and I are both motivated to do this deal. Why do we need a default clause in the offer?
- What are some default remedies that should appear in a contract.
- What other people might I need to hire to assist me with buying and closing on property?

The choice of whether to work with a real estate agent or not will depend on your own particular skills, philosophy, and budgeting. As a general rule, I recommend a real estate agent because I believe he or she will help you be more efficient, avoid mistakes, and remain emotionally detached and rational regarding negotiations. If you elect to work without a real estate agent, you will need to do more legwork and be better prepared with things like forms and checklists.

What are the pros and cons of buying property without a real estate agent?

Pros:

- You may be able to save money by offering lower acceptable prices to sellers.

- As you work your way through obtaining information about many different properties, the education will help you be a smarter and more efficient shopper. Often, you will accidentally learn about things that might change your investment strategy. Working with a real estate agent is often like doing a Google or Yahoo search—if you ask a precise question, you will receive a precise answer. Search engines do not volunteer other things you might want to think about.

- You will search a wider variety of sources than a real estate agent for a longer period of time. Selling real estate is a business, not a hobby. Agents cannot afford to spend vast amounts of time with you while you find the perfect investment. At some point, they need to cut their losses and move on to other things. You will not get discouraged so easily because it is your own investment.

- Many good investments are owned by sellers who have not previously thought about selling. Catch someone on the landlord's equivalent of a bad hair day, and he or she might be willing to sell his or her property to you on the spot, and hold 100% of the financing.

Cons:

- The learning curve is enormous. Books like this can help, but there are many localized and time-sensitive issues that cannot be covered in a book with a nationwide audience. How do you find properties? Who is the best property inspector? What local regulations will affect how I can use my property? What are the market rents? What is a fair price?

- A very large amount of your time will be spent on unproductive activities, such as looking at info blurbs on three hundred properties that do not meet your investment requirements. You will play phone tag with listing agents and then discover their property is already under contract or out of your price range. Finding the right investment properties is a time-consuming chore.

- You will have no forms, no checklists, and no advice unless you find those resources yourself by spending the necessary time.

- Many people cannot emotionally distance themselves from negotiations. They feel threatened by even the mildest form of confrontation or rejection. Some buyers do not want to insult sellers by making offers substantially less than the asking price. Others have buyers' remorse—they readily agree to things and then regret the agreements afterward. All of those people need to school themselves to do better, or hire an agent.

Can I find Multiple Listing Service (MLS) properties if I do not have an agent?

Many local real estate agents have links on their websites to area MLS listings for all companies, not just their own. You can browse the listings, or do some limited searches, and then contact the listing agents directly for more information.

What are other ways to find real estate for sale?

Be aware that many commercial properties are not listed on MLS. There are some nationwide listing sites such as LoopNet at **www.loopnet.com** that offer free search capabilities. CoStar Commercial MLS, at **www.costar.com**, provides inexpensive monthly packages for access to listings. Any number of other sites have for-sale-by-owner information, local broker listings, and regional information. You will have to search until you find the websites that seem most useful for your purposes. The National Association of REALTORS® estimates that 87% of all buyers find their information on the Internet, so you are in good company!

> **Tip:** The most productive way you can find deals is to get out and look in areas you like. Drive up and down those streets. Look on grocery store bulletin boards for FSBO ads. Yes, it is time-consuming and often boring. But, you can stumble across some real gems while gaining an intensive education about the entire area.

Will sellers take me seriously if I do not have an agent?

How you conduct yourself will largely determine your credibility. Are you confident, knowledgeable, and straightforward in your conversations? Do you have a good idea of what you want and what you like about a particular property? These things are important, but not deadly if you do not have them.

You should invest in some business cards, even if they are the kind you print yourself on specialized office supply store paper. Without the card, someone will probably lose your contact information after they write it on a scrap of paper. It is a little thing, but business cards say that you *are* in business—that you are serious about your investing.

Will a seller reduce his or her price if I don't have an agent representing me?

Often, a seller will reduce his or her price if the seller's agent will reduce his or commission. In a typical transaction for $100,000 and a 6% commission, the listing broker will make $6,000 and the seller will net $94,000. The listing agent will almost always agree to split that commission equally with another broker if the other broker brings the buyer to the closing table. As a result, on this transaction the listing broker will make $3,000 and the selling broker will make $3,000. The listing broker may be willing to reduce his or her commission to only 3% if he or she does not have to split it with anyone else. Your offer could then say, "I offer to pay $97,000 purchase price, with the listing agent to receive $3,000 and no selling agent involved." The listing agent receives the same fee he or she would if you had an agent. The seller receives the same net amount he or she would otherwise. You save $3,000. Everyone is happy.

How do I make an offer?

When you are fairly comfortable that conversations and negotiations have given you enough information to make an offer, you should put it in writing. This allows you time to think about all the things *besides price* that should be included in your offer. It avoids misunderstandings because the other party can always refer back to your written offer instead of his or her perhaps faulty memory. In most states, real estate agents are required to submit written offers to their clients immediately, but may sit on verbal offers until something better comes in. Finally, a written offer requires only the seller's signature to make it a binding contract. That efficiency is usually important to all parties.

Ask real estate agents and lawyers if they will share with you any offer forms they have. Look on the Internet, and in forms books and office supply stores. While it is a lot of reading, you want to start building a checklist of things that should be in your own, personalized offers. Remember that investment properties are normally going to require more agreed-upon items than a typical home sale. Refer to chapters regarding specific property types for things you might want to cover in an offer.

Your offer should be simple. It can consist of bullet points or complete paragraphs. It should say, at the beginning, "This is the parties' agreement." Here are some standard things that all offers should address:

- property address
- legal description
- names of ALL owners
- name of buyer
- buyer can assign contract
- price
- earnest money
- seller financing
- terms of financing
- closing costs split
- due diligence
- contingencies
- possession
- encumbrances
- what happens if one party defaults

Some of these are discussed in the following sections.

Why do I want to require that the contract is assignable?

If you sign a purchase contract in your own name, you might want the closing in the name of a corporation, partnership, or something similar. For investments over a certain size, many lenders will require you to set up a special *single asset entity* to hold title to the real estate. Or, someone might offer you a healthy profit just to flip the property before you even close!

Is earnest money required?

Earnest money is not technically necessary for an enforceable real estate contract. Most buyers will require some amount of earnest money, but that is not true 100% of the time. You can find opportunities to buy property with no cash outlay until the day of closing.

If you promise to buy, and the seller promises to sell, that is enough for an enforceable contract. Many buyers mistakenly assume they can freely cancel a contract if they never wrote the earnest money check. Many sellers mistakenly believe they can change their mind if they simply do not cash the earnest money check. Neither of these things is true.

Earnest money shows that you have some financial resources and can afford to pay. It also has hostage value, so that you will think twice before changing your mind and forfeiting it. Although earnest money is not essential for an enforceable contract, it can in some circumstances indicate that a contract exists. For example, if several counteroffers go back and forth, the seller might not think to initial the last set. Technically, no contract exists until the seller formally accepts your last counteroffer. But, if the seller accepts and cashes your earnest money check, that can suffice to cure the technical defect.

How much earnest money should I offer?

If money is tight, you might want to omit any earnest money from your offer. Odds are, the seller will request something. That number might be less than you would have offered to start with.

The amount of earnest money will vary greatly among deals. There is no set percentage or rule of thumb. If the seller has not had any offers that are even close to acceptable, it will take only a small amount of earnest money to convince him or her you are a serious buyer. Hot markets may require larger earnest money deposits. Just remember, as much as you think you know about that property, as perfect as you think it might be, something could happen to change your mind. You have to be willing to forfeit whatever amount you offer, in case it becomes necessary.

What should I put in the seller financing part of the offer?

Read Chapter 23. The courts will not enforce a seller-financing agreement if the parties have not specified enough terms in advance for the court to create a note and a mortgage. This does not mean you must agree on all the boilerplate stuff—just the important terms in the chapter on that subject.

What is due diligence?

Due diligence has been defined as "the process of investigating all facts, conditions, rules, laws, regulations, financial considerations, or any other such matters as would affect one's decision to purchase property." These things will differ depending on the type of property you wish to buy. They will be discussed in greater detail in chapters devoted to specific property types.

If you were buying a home, you would normally reserve the right to cancel without penalty upon the happening of certain contingencies—failure to obtain satisfactory financing, failure to sell your own home, property does not pass its inspections, etc. When buying investment properties, there are just too many things that could ruin the deal. Many of them will not even occur to you until one question leads to another and then another, until you possibly reach a roadblock. That is why many commercial contracts provide only a general due diligence clause.

A *general due diligence* clause says you can check anything you need to check. At the end of an agreed-upon time period, it is time to fish or cut bait. You notify the seller that you are proceeding to closing, or that you are cancelling the contract and wish a return of your earnest money.

> **Note:** A word of caution—many items of due diligence take far more time than you would think. If a property is not already zoned for your use, a final decision on a zoning variance could take many months. Other professionals, such as surveyors and engineers, may have tight schedules and not be able to work your job in until weeks away. Be sure to leave yourself enough time to check all potential problems. If in doubt about how long this might be, ask advice from other investors in similar properties, or from your lender.

Read Chapter 20 on due diligence to learn about specific things you should check before making your final commitment to buy the property. The point at which you confirm that your due diligence checks out and you will proceed to closing is called *going hard*. When talking to a lender or to friends, you might say, "I am going to let the contract go hard on Friday." It means that the earnest money will not be refunded if you change your mind, and it will be "hard" to get out of the contract after that point.

I have a due diligence clause. Why do I also need a contingencies clause?

The *contingencies clause* is for surprises that come up *after* you have done all the due diligence you can. Some people like to put a financing contingency in their contracts because negotiating financing can be very lengthy with a commercial transaction. I usually have only a title contingency—if it turns out that the seller does not have clear title for some reason, then I can cancel. That might be because the seller has a spouse I did not know about, but must sign the deed for me to get 100% title to the property. If the success of the deal depends on something happening in the future, you might want to include that as a contingency.

What are encumbrances?

An *encumbrance* is something that places a claim or burden on property. Mortgages are encumbrances that must be paid off at closing in order to deliver good title. Leases are also encumbrances. If a seller leases some or all of the property to someone else before closing, then you might be saddled for many years with a tenant you do not want, at below-market prices. You should require in your offer that the seller disclose to you all leases—including billboard, mineral, air rights, and premises—currently on the property or under negotiation. *Easements* should also be disclosed—these are rights to do something on the property (right of way, parking) or to avoid doing something (scenic view easement.) Your encumbrance clause wants to provide that the seller will not enter into any agreements affecting the property after the date of your offer, unless they are disclosed to you and agreed upon by you in writing.

The seller and I are both motivated to do this deal. Why do we need a default clause in the offer?

Because things happen. You buy insurance because you might suffer financially crippling surprises. You put a default clause in a contract for the same reason.

What are some default remedies that should appear in a contract?

If the seller refuses to go through with closing, the buyer can often force that result through something called a *specific performance lawsuit*. But, the buyer has to spend legal fees. Not all states automatically allow the buyer to recover those fees, so the contract has to say the parties agree to it.

If the seller defaults but cannot deliver good title if he or she wanted, or if the buyer elects to demand specific performance, then the buyer should be reimbursed for his or her out-of-pocket expenses for due diligence and loan commitments. That seems reasonable. Many buyers want to collect damages for their lost profits on the deal, and so do not want to limit their agreement to the aforementioned matters. In my experience, it is virtually impossible for a small investor or a new investor to collect lost profits. The courts rule that any profits are just too speculative. Plus, the illusion of being able to collect this money often leads you down the primrose path of massive expenditures in legal fees, time, and emotional turmoil. I recommend you move on with your life and find some other investment.

If the buyer defaults, the seller usually keeps the earnest money but agrees not to sue the buyer for any other damages. Those could potentially be very large, especially if the seller later accepts a much lower offer. You might be liable for the difference in the two prices, plus interest. In one very unusual circumstance in California, a seller was able to force the buyer to go through with closing. If you are the buyer, agree to give up the earnest money and reimburse the seller for any out-of-pocket expenses associated with getting ready to move out, make repairs you requested, or do other such things.

What other people might I need to hire to assist me with buying and closing on property?

Depending on the investment, you might need inspectors, engineers, attorneys, and appraisers, to name a few. The best way to employ each of these professionals is discussed in the next chapter.

Chapter 17

HIRING PROFESSIONALS— WORK EFFICIENTLY BY HIRING THE BEST

- Will I need a surveyor?
- Why do I need an appraisal?
- How can an inspector save me money on my commercial property?
- I am not building bridges. Why do I need an engineer?
- Can I hire a real estate consultant?

As a real estate investor, you will have a need to find, hire, and manage a wide variety of professionals. This is an introduction to the most common types. You will find out why you might need them and resources for finding the best ones for your situation.

Will I need a surveyor?

Depending on the size of your investment and your plans to build, many lenders will require a survey. It is always a good idea to obtain one, though.

A surveyor can do something as simple as marking property corners to something as complex as scale drawings of the real estate, all improvements upon it, the changes in *slope* (rises and falls in the terrain), and anything a neighboring property owner has erroneously placed on the land under consideration, or vice versa. When one owner's improvements are completely or partially on someone else's land, that is called an *encroachment*. I once had a neighbor who built his house almost completely on his next-door neighbor's land. No one knew where the boundary lines were. Five years later, after a total expenditure of $50,000 in legal fees, surveyors, separate court-ordered appraisers, depositions, and other expenses, a judge ruled that the property line ran through the garage. The judge ordered the neighbor who actually owned the property to sell some of the land to the other person—enough for the house and a tiny amount of side yard. You want to avoid such problems. A survey is relatively cheap compared to potential court costs later on.

I recommend a survey if you are buying anything more than a subdivision lot. As I mentioned, boundary line disputes between neighbors can be extremely costly. In most circumstances there is no insurance coverage for the legal fees and potential liability unless you obtained a specific, seldom-ordered endorsement to your title insurance policy. In that case, the only way you will be able to buy that endorsement is if you have a survey.

If you plan on building improvements on land, you might want to order a *topographic survey* (changes in slope) so you will be able to calculate if you need any fill dirt for the low places or cutting down of the high places. You may also have to satisfy regulatory requirements regarding storm water control. To do that, you will need a drawing that shows where the water flows naturally.

For more information, check out the website of LandSurveyor.US LLC at **www.landsurveyor.us**. The site has some excellent articles and responses to frequently asked questions. It also contains links to other sites, including specialized ones for each state.

Why do I need an appraisal?

Virtually every loan in the United States must now be supported by an appraisal of the property value because of federal lending regulations. Due to abuses in the past, the borrower is not allowed to have any input into the appraisal process, for fear of influencing the outcome. On the other hand, if you have information about recent sales prices of comparable properties, you should share that with your lender. The information will probably make its way to the appraiser as part of the data he or she considers in arriving at a value.

If I am selling a property, I always like to obtain an appraisal. It serves as a reality check, to see if I am accurate in my own estimate of value. The appraisal also provides tremendous negotiating leverage for me. If a potential buyer argues about the price I have set for the property, I can show him or her the appraisal. While it will not help you with the bottom fishers, who always want to buy properties for less than their value, it will assist you with people who truly believe the property is worth less than its asking price but are willing to be educated otherwise. It also gives them confidence that their lender will provide the necessary financing, at that price.

The Appraisal Institute has some very good consumer brochures at **www.appraisalinstitute.org/resources/brochures.asp**. It offers two designations. The MAI is the highest designation. It requires a college degree, 380 hours of appraisal instruction with a passing score on all 11 exams, a passing score on a two-day comprehensive exam, and 4,500 hours of experience. An SRA designation for residential appraisers and the SRPA for commercial property appraisers have much less stringent requirements.

How can an inspector save me money on my commercial property?

We have all heard of home inspectors, but the same services are usually necessary for commercial properties, as well. Typically, a commercial property inspector will be an engineer or someone with more training and experience than the average home inspector. That is because there is such a wide variety of commercial properties, and such a huge range of defects and problems, that more knowledge and skill is necessary for them.

For buyers, the inspector discovers property defects that could affect the buying decision, or at least the offering price.

> **Example:** A friend of mine once bought a small office building without first hiring an inspector. He thought he did not need one because the building was relatively new, and the seller was also the builder, and a very experienced one at that.
>
> One year later my friend needed to make some changes to the electrical system. Those changes required a building permit and a building inspection. The inspectors discovered that the entire building's electrical system was defective because it was not wired

to electrical code requirements. There were rumors of payoffs that enabled the first owner to pass the original inspection. The city ordered my friend to remove all tenants from the premises, rewire the entire building, and only after passing a final inspection would he be allowed to rent offices again. He lost a tremendous amount of revenue, had to pay tens of thousands of dollars for electrical work, and nearly went bankrupt. All of that because he did not pay $500 for an inspection report.

Sellers can benefit from an inspection because it usually alerts them to relatively minor problems that can be fixed inexpensively. Afterward, the seller can obtain an updated—clean—inspection report. That always provides a high degree of comfort for potential buyers, and helps reinforce the asking price of the property.

The American Society of Home Inspectors offers consumer guides, virtual inspections, and directories at its website, **www.ashi.org**. I could find nothing similar for commercial inspectors. A local engineer or the construction-permitting department of your community might be able to offer you guidance and some names.

I am not building bridges. Why do I need an engineer?

A building with evidence of settling—cracks in the exterior or interior walls or gaps between the building and sidewalks or steps—should be checked out by a structural engineer. You want to know if it has typical minor settling associated with age, if you have construction weaknesses, or if sinkholes are developing beneath the building.

An engineer can also advise you regarding relatively easy ways to solve water problems that might be depressing the value of a property.

Example: Another friend of mine, a retired engineer, bought a house that suffered water damage every time there was a hard rain. The former owner installed an elaborate drain system that did not work. My friend bought the house for a big discount. Afterward, he had two dump truck loads of fill dirt delivered to raise the ground level slightly at the house. Afterward, rain water coming off the roof, and from other parts of the property, drained toward the street instead of toward the house. Problem solved! It seems simple once someone explains it, but the prior owner was not trained to see such easy solutions.

If you plan to develop property as an investment, the engineer will advise you regarding environmental requirements for storm water runoff. Installation of a storm sewer system, or construction of a retention pond, injection well, artificial wetlands, or such, could change the economics of your project. Lenders for development projects will require that you provide a *Phase I Environmental Report*, available from a licensed engineer. It discloses the likelihood of any hazardous waste on the property, based on the historical uses of the property and interviews with knowledgeable people.

The American Society of Civil Engineers' website at **www.asce.org** has additional information and resources for you.

Can I hire a real estate consultant?

Real estate consulting is becoming a more established and respected profession. A real estate consultant can give you a terrific general education regarding tax advantages to investing, hot markets in your community, local lender attitudes to various investments, and good ratios or rules of thumb to use when creating your financial projections.

Some consultants charge by the hour, and others by the job. As with any professional, have a clear agreement regarding what services you will receive, which services are not covered by the agreement, and what it will cost.

> **Tip:** The National Association of Real Estate Consultants website at **www.narec.com** is a good starting place for learning about such people, what they have to offer, and locating licensed consultants in your city or town.

Chapter 18

WHAT SHOULD I PAY?—A CRASH COURSE ON APPRAISAL TECHNIQUES YOU CAN MASTER

- How do I find a house exactly like mine so I can see what price the other one brought when it was sold?
- Where do I find sales prices of homes?
- How do I find information about sales prices for business properties?
- How do I adjust for differences between recently sold properties and the residential property I want to buy or sell?
- How do I value business property once I know the amount of comparable sales?
- What are per-unit values?
- How can I use the gross rent multiplier?
- All the real estate brokers I know talk about NOI. What is that?
- How do I find the right cap rate?
- Can you give an example of cap rates affecting property values?
- Under what circumstances would I use a discounted cash flow method to value property?
- How do I calculate the discounted cash flow for a property?
- I know what I want to pay for an investment. How do I convince the seller to sell at that price?

Paying too much for a property is one of the most common causes of investment failure. If you pay too much, the rents you are able to charge will not support the purchase price. Purchasers who buy in order to resell will not be able to recover their costs, much less make a profit.

Evaluating the right purchase price is critical. We are going to learn several methods employed by professional appraisers. You will not have the experience or the access to information to replace an appraiser, and you will not have the analytical tools to fine-tune your evaluation. You will, however, be pretty close to the money.

How do I find a house exactly like mine so I can see what price the other one brought when it was sold?

Short answer: You cannot find such a property. You must find *comparable properties*—"comps" for short—that are reasonably similar to the one you want to buy or to sell.

To do that, you need a list of the core qualities of your property, so you can find other properties with very similar core qualities. Those differ among types of property. For a residence, it might be the number of bedrooms and bathrooms, number of stories, type of exterior siding, age of the house, and general quality of the neighborhood.

You find those properties by reading the real estate magazines for your area, searching the online MLS databases, and by going around neighborhoods. First attention should be given to those properties with "Sold" signs. The selling price is the best indication of value, not the asking price. Before a property sells, you know only the asking price. Real estate still being offered for sale will give you clues about neighborhoods to research. Houses within a neighborhood are usually very similar to each other. If a house is for sale, look for nearby houses that sold in the last two years.

Where do I find sales prices of homes?

Your local real estate tax assessor usually keeps track of the sales price of properties. Many states require people to declare the purchase price when they record their deeds. That information is then given to the tax assessor, or it might also be available to the public from the recorder of deeds. Call or visit those two offices for your county or parish and ask them how the public can access that information. Generally, it is available online and at terminals in the government office.

> **Tip:** If you have a friend who is a real estate agent, he or she can help you with MLS information. The publicly available MLS databases include only properties currently for sale. The professional versions allow members to research sales prices of properties, as well.

How do I find information about sales prices for business properties?

Finding information about sales prices for business properties is more difficult than for homes and condos because there is usually no centralized location for sales information. In fact, you will often not even see a "For Sale" sign on property that is offered to the market because the owners are afraid their current or potential customers might misinterpret it and think they are going out of business.

You will need to be very attentive to your marketplace in order to discover recent sales of business properties. Some local weekly business journals list all recent commercial real estate sales. You might be able to monitor this on your tax assessor's website, if you can do a search on *non-homestead property*. This is property that is not owner-occupied, so the owner did not declare a homestead exemption that would reduce his or her taxes. Talk to real estate professionals and lenders to keep track of what is for sale and what has sold recently. When driving around, look for signs of change. A new business at an existing location means a new tenant or a new owner. Investigate further.

How do I adjust for differences between recently sold properties and the residential property I want to buy or sell?

This is the true art and skill of an appraiser. He or she usually first obtains the sales prices of three properties that are as close to yours as possible that sold within the last two years.

Next, the appraiser makes adjustments. If Home #1 is exactly like yours except that it has a two-car garage and you have only a two-car covered carport, then the appraiser must adjust the sales price of Home #1 accordingly. If that home sold for $145,000, the appraiser might say, "That price is partially because of the garage. I think the garage added $5,000 worth of increased value over a carport. I am going to adjust the price downward to $140,000. If Home #1 had a carport, like the one I am appraising, it probably would have sold for only $140,000."

If that is true, then your house is worth $140,000. The appraiser makes a series of adjustments, some upward and some downward, until he or she is comfortable with placing a value on your home.

The glaring problem for you is, how do you know how much that garage is worth? How do you know how much to adjust the sales price? If an appraiser will share that general information with you, do not be bashful about asking. That is easier if you are trying to buy something because he or she knows you must obtain a *real* appraisal in order to obtain a loan.

If you are selling, appraisers will not want to share their information with you. You should hire a professional appraiser instead of trying to do it yourself. It will more than pay for itself in setting the right price, gaining credibility with buyers, and making the loan approval process faster for purchasers.

How do I value business property once I know the amount of comparable sales?

Generally speaking, business properties have sales prices based on a *per-unit* amount or based on something called the *Net Operating Income* (NOI) and the *capitalization rate* (cap rate) or sometimes based on the *discounted cash flow*. We will address all of these. They sound pretty complicated, but once someone explains the concepts, they will make sense and be easy for you to duplicate.

What are per-unit values?

Many investors save time by using a rule of thumb to screen through many opportunities. It is not the most accurate method of analysis, but it will tell you if you want to spend more time evaluating the property more thoroughly. The *per-unit value* is one rule of thumb. Within any community, investors will know approximately what things are worth by reference to how many rentable units it has and the going price per unit.

For example, apartment complexes are often compared based on a price per apartment, for somewhat similar sized complexes. Four-unit and six-unit apartment buildings might have sales prices that work out to $85,000 per unit. Larger complexes have different economies of scale and are attractive to different buyers, so the price per unit might be $120,000. Small, non-climate controlled, self-storage facilities with an average unit size of 100 square feet might sell for $3,000 per unit. Hotel and motel prices typically work out to a certain amount per rentable room. You simply take the per-unit price, multiply it by your number of units, and arrive at something close to a value.

How can I use the gross rent multiplier?

Some people use a rule of thumb called the *gross rent multiplier*. This is not very precise, but it helps them make buying decisions very efficiently. The actual ratios vary among markets. One example might be: "I will not buy any property unless I can buy it for no more than the monthly rent times 100." If the monthly rent you think you can charge is $900, then you will pay up to $90,000 to buy the property, and no more. You will need to talk to other investors to find out the rule of thumb for your marketplace. Be aware that this is a very unsophisticated measurement. You may overlook some excellent opportunities if you employ only the gross rent multiplier to make decisions. On the other hand, a commonly used, conservative gross rent multiplier will rarely land you in trouble with a poor purchase.

All the real estate brokers I know talk about NOI. What is that?

The *Net Operating Income* (NOI) method of evaluation is much more precise than the Gross Rent Multiplier method. Start by taking the gross annual income from a property. Some sellers like to play games, and say, "*My* gross annual income is $60,000, but if *you* raised the rents, did a better job of keeping vacancies down, and installed a laundromat, *your* gross annual income could be $95,000." That $95,000 is called *pro forma* income. You want the numbers for *actual* income. Real estate agents will sometimes tell you, "The pro forma NOI is $95,000" or even, "That purchase price is an 8% cap on pro forma NOI." Any time you see the words "pro forma" you should think "wishful thinking." Those numbers might come true, as with a new development still filling up, or they might never come true.

After obtaining the income, subtract all the *annual operating expenses*, which are things like taxes, insurance, management fees, repairs and maintenance, marketing expenses, leasing commissions, and utilities. Anything you spend on that property, except mortgage payments, is an operating expense. See Appendix C for a worksheet to help you.

When researching comparable properties, you can usually estimate the gross annual income from the rents being charged in the building and get a good idea of the vacancy rate. Lenders can usually tell you ratios for operating expenses, such as that apartment complex operating expenses are going to be 27% of gross potential rent. Gross potential rent is what revenues you would have if the property were 100% leased up. Most operating expenses are fixed— they do not rise and fall as occupancies rise and fall. That is why operating expenses are estimated as a percentage of gross potential rent, not as a percentage of actual rents.

Subtract annual operating expenses from annual rent. The figure you obtain is called the Net Operating Income (NOI). You divide the NOI by the capitalization rate—*cap rate*—to obtain a value. If you have an NOI of $8,100, and the cap rate is 11%, then $8,100 ÷ 0.11 = $73,636. The property is worth $73,636. Someone might argue with the choice of cap rate, but the NOI is what it is. In the prior example, if you used a cap rate of 10%, the value would increase to $81,000. If you used a cap rate of 12%, the value would decrease to $67,500.

How do I find the right cap rate?

Cap rates are market driven. They change depending on loan interest rates, the quality of property and its tenants, and demand for that particular type of property. You will have to ask lenders and experienced investors what the current cap rates are. If you can subscribe to specialized magazines or e-zines for your particular type of property, do so. They will usually have information about prevailing sales prices nationwide and current cap rates.

Generally speaking, as the quality of a property and its tenants decline in relation to what is considered first class, the cap rate will increase. That seems counterintuitive, but think about it this way: if you were going to invest cash to buy real estate, what kind of return would you want on your money, considering the risk you are taking regarding the quality of the tenants, the possibility of future major repairs, or the possibility of market changes decreasing your rents? The riskier the property, the higher return you would want. You might want 12% on your money for a run-down strip center with a high turnover in tenants. You might be happy with 5% on your money for a brand-new strip center with tenants like Subway, FedEx/Kinkos, and a branch bank, all of which have twenty-year leases and annual rent increases. The higher return you must earn on your purchase price money, the less you can afford to spend. Cap rates work in the same manner.

Can you give an example of cap rates affecting property values?

Think about wanting a higher return on your investment if it has a lot of risk. Suppose you are willing to buy something in a depressed part of town, but you want to earn 15% on your money. For purposes of these calculations, we consider "your" down payment and the bank's borrowed funds as all being "your" money. That is because if the rents are insufficient to make the mortgage payments, you will have to do so.

You want a 15% return on your money. The NOI is $8,100. The rest is simple algebra. You probably remember the formula from grammar school. It goes like this: 15 has the same ratio to 100 as $8,100 has to what number? That number is the purchase price. In other words, $8,100 a year is 15% of what number?

$$\frac{15}{100} = \frac{8,100}{X}$$

To solve for "X" you multiply 8,100 times 100 and then divide by 15. The answer is 54,000. If you invest $54,000 and earn $8,100 per year, you will earn 15% on your money.

If you are willing to earn only 9% on your money, then the same calculations will give you the following:

$$\frac{9}{100} = \frac{8,100}{X}$$

To solve for "X" you multiply 8,100 times 100 and then divide by 9. The answer is 90,000. If you invest $90,000 and earn $8,100 per year, you will earn 9% on your money.

This is the idea behind NOI and cap rates. The property is more valuable, in relation to its annual income, if you are willing to have a smaller percentage return on your money.

Under what circumstances would I use a discounted cash flow method to value property?

Net Operating Income (NOI) is, by definition, dependant on operations. In other words, use that method if there are some expenses associated with owning and operating the property. If you have only cash income with no expenses, such as NNN leases (see Chapter 13), then you use *discounted cash flow* to value the property.

Discounted cash flow means: "What would someone pay today in order to receive a steady stream of income over some period of time?" That analysis requires you to decide how much risk is involved with the stream of income stopping earlier than antici- pated, and how long it will take you to earn all your money back.

If the money is coming from an NNN lease with Wal-Mart as a tenant, you are probably fairly confident you will receive all your rent payments for the next thirty years. You would have a small risk, so you would be willing to accept a modest return on your money, maybe 5%. If the money is coming from an NNN lease with "Uncle Charlie's BBQ Pit," you might think there was a greater possibility of default and want to earn a higher return, maybe around 15%. Every investor must make those decisions for him- or herself.

When a lender loans money to you, he or she thinks: "I am going to loan out $100,000 today and be repaid over the next twenty years. What interest rate do I want to earn in order to be willing to do that?" If you have good credit, you will receive a lower interest rate. If you have terrible credit, you will be charged a higher interest rate. Short-term loans usually have lower interest rates than long- term loans. If the lender thought in terms of discounted cash flow, he or she might say, "Someone is willing to pay me $733.76 per month for the next thirty years. The total of those payments will be $264,153. If I want to earn 8% interest on my money, how much will I loan him or her today so that all the payments, over time, will result in 8% annual interest?" The answer is $100,000.

How do I calculate the discounted cash flow for a property?

The calculations are a little more time-consuming than most people want to take on. They are easy, but have many steps. I recommend using one of the excellent online calculators to perform this chore. One of the easiest to use is on the website of a company called Money Toys. It has many different financial calculators, and it sells the online calculators to other people, such as real estate agents, to install on their own websites. There is no charge, however, to use the calculator on the Money Toys website. The address is:

www.moneytoys.com/cash-flow-calculator.php

I know what I want to pay for an investment. How do I convince the seller to sell at that price?

A few simple negotiation skills are usually all you need to success-fully purchase properties at a reasonable price. Nothing is guaranteed—some sellers are completely hardheaded—but you improve your odds as you improve your persuasive abilities. Read the following chapter for insights into the art of negotiation.

Chapter 19

NEGOTIATION— POWER TIPS FOR POWER RESULTS

■ How do I find out what motivates someone?

■ I cannot have a conversation with the seller because he or she is represented by an agent, who is more careful in what he or she says. How do I find out what motivates the seller?

■ What seller motivations do I want to find out?

■ I am afraid of insulting a seller by offering a low price. How do I handle that?

■ How do I avoid misunderstandings during the ebb-and-flow of negotiations?

■ What is a good format for my letter of intent?

■ What is the most useful negotiating device, in your opinion?

■ How can I learn more about successful negotiations?

■ After I negotiate the deal, what comes next?

Any successful investor will tell you that negotiating skills can add immeasurably to your success. There is no secret to mastering that ability. Much of it involves listening and making a response that addresses the other person's needs.

The following is a true story. A prime piece of undeveloped real estate was owned by an elderly woman. The land was at the best intersection of the highest per-capita income area in six counties. One road of the intersection was a super highway that could easily deliver shoppers from nearby states. Hundreds of acres sat there, covered in trees and nothing else. Every developer in five states wanted the property, but no one could convince the woman to sell.

A friend of mine went to visit the lady. She lived on the land, a short way back from the road. They drank tea and ate cookies, chatting away the afternoon. They talked about the weather, the quality of store-bought cookies, and the problems with raccoons getting into your garbage. Everything except real estate. Finally, my friend said something along the lines of, "Everyone wonders why you don't sell this land for the millions and millions of dollars you've been offered, and move to someplace equally beautiful but without the traffic noise all the time. Why is that?"

The woman replied, "I know those people want to bulldoze all the trees and build a shopping center. My family cemetery is on the top of that little peak over there. I can't allow them to be moved. They deserve their peace." My friend answered, "After you're gone, your heirs will do exactly that. You know they will. If you'll sell the land to me now, I'll fence off a five-acre area around the cemetery, leave it wooded and natural, and maintain it as a bird and wildlife sanctuary forever. If I did that, would you sell the land to me?"

The woman agreed, my friend delivered on his promise, and he built a regional lifestyle center with every high-end retailer you can imagine. He did not have much money at the time, but he had that land tied up, and was able to choose among a long list of investors who wanted in on the deal.

That is the power of negotiation. There is nothing tricky to it—find a solution that meets everyone's needs.

How do I find out what motivates someone?

You listen. You might ask, point-blank:

- This seems like a great property. Why are you selling?
- What do you plan to do after the sale?
- I'm sure other investors have approached you and asked you to sell. What didn't you like about them or their offers?
- I'm a new investor. Do you have any advice you'd be willing to share with me?

Sellers also might ask:

- What first caught your attention about the property I'm selling?
- Just in case this property is not right for you, I might have access to some other things. What does your wish list have on it?

Very rarely will the direct response to your question give you enough information to negotiate successfully. Prompt the other person to expand on his or her comments. You never know where a conversation is going to lead. Be patient. That is probably the hardest part in negotiation.

I cannot have a conversation with the seller because he or she is represented by an agent, who is more careful in what he or she says. How do I find out what motivates the seller?

You listen to the agent, and you do some research on your own. Agents will often tell you a lot regarding the seller's plans, especially if you ask direct questions. I have found over the years that a direct question, delivered in a confident manner as if you fully expected a direct answer, will yield results 99% of the time. Do not start with the hard questions, though. Start with questions that are completely innocent. You want the other side to get in the habit of answering you. In other words, you want it to feel like a conversation, not an interview in front of the *60 Minutes* cameras.

The real estate records in your community may reveal if the seller has any financial pressures, such as owning two homes and needing to sell one, IRS liens, or creditor judgments. Even a simple Google search on the Internet can yield surprising results.

What seller motivations do I want to find out?

If you have very little cash and a slim-to-none chance of borrowing money, you want a landlord-seller who is motivated to receive his or her same regular income from his or her property but is fed up with dealing with tenant headaches. Meet his or her needs by buying the property with seller financing, and you have a deal. If you are meeting someone's needs, even if it works out tremendously to your advantage, never apologize or feel reluctant to do the deal.

Other seller motivations might include a willingness to sell at a reasonable price, but only if the seller can obtain another investment. Some have unreasonably high prices because of what they need to make in order to pay other bills, not what the property is actually worth. Talk to them, help them solve their other problems in a more creative way, and you can make a deal. Many, many sellers want a buyer who will love their property and take care of it. These are very emotional decisions. The more you can communicate your plans and enlist their buy-in, the more successful you will be.

I am afraid of insulting a seller by offering a low price. How do I handle that?

Sometimes, negotiations depend on creating an emotional response in the other person. Emotional responses play an important role in negotiations, which is why you are wise to worry about insulting sellers.

You might say, "I really love your property, but in order to make the numbers work on this investment, your asking price will make the deal impossible. It's nothing about you or your property, but this offer is the most I can justify under the circumstances." This approach avoids insulting the seller and enlists his or her aid in making your numbers work. Perhaps the seller knows something that might make your financial analysis different. Perhaps not. Either way, you have taken the emotion out of the situation.

How do I avoid misunderstandings during the ebb-and-flow of negotiations?

You have seen lawyers negotiating a settlement on television. They face each other across a conference table. One of them grabs a piece of paper and scribbles a dollar amount on it. He or she folds the paper and slides it carefully across the table. The other one sneaks a peak at the number, and then scribbles another one and slides the paper back. This goes on for several minutes until they agree. High drama, but it illustrates a point.

Put the deal points in writing. After that slip of paper finishes its journey back and forth across the conference table, some other lawyers in the firm will spend the next three days drafting the ninety-two-page settlement agreement. Most of it will be boiler-plate. The deal almost never falls apart in haggling over the boilerplate, once the parties agree on the deal points.

The mechanism for this is the *letter of intent*. At the top, it should say, "This is not a contract. This illustrates the current stage of negotiations only." That way, you do not find yourself accidentally locked into a contract because of some legal technicality you did not know about. Write the date and the time at the top, also, in case you have several versions floating around. Never destroy earlier versions. They are good proof regarding what the parties discussed, agreed upon, and rejected. That might become important later. You never know.

What is a good format for my letter of intent?

The best way to write a letter of intent is to have a list of important points, with blanks next to each of them. Do not worry about any pretty language or narrative. That is for the lawyers to worry about.

You fill in the blanks on the letter of intent as you talk and come to an agreement on each issue. At the end, if everyone is in agreement, you draw up a formal contract, or just strike out the language that says, "This is not a contract" and write in, "This is the parties' contract." Everybody signs at the bottom.

What is the most useful negotiating device, in your opinion?

I think the most useful negotiating device is the one called *third partying it out*. This means that whatever problems there are in coming to an agreement, whatever thing you cannot agree to, you say, "I see your point there, but my (partner, spouse, lender, whoever) will not agree to that. I'll ask him or her, but I don't think there will be any surprises." This takes the emotion out of the situation. Everything is someone else's fault. The two people negotiating are still buddies, still working on a deal. This mechanism also buys you time to think, because you have to run things past your (partner, spouse, lender, whoever).

How can I learn more about successful negotiations?

There are many, many inexpensive seminars, DVDs, and CDs on this subject, as well as books and magazine articles. They all discuss variants of about twelve different techniques that you can easily master. You should invest in one of those resources. I prefer CDs because I can listen to them in my car. As you encounter different situations and gain more experience, some of the techniques will become more relevant to you. The ability to refresh that education, several times over during your investing career, can be extremely valuable.

After I negotiate the deal, what comes next?

The next step is going to be your *due diligence*—making sure there are no surprises. You should also work on your financing at the same time. An inability to borrow enough money might be your biggest surprise. Do not wait until the very end to find out.

Chapter 20

Due Diligence— Avoiding Surprises

■ How detailed should the due diligence clause be in a purchase contract?
■ Besides a property inspection, what else do I need for due diligence?
■ How can I find due diligence checklists so I know what to check?
■ Is securing my loan part of due diligence?

The process of *due diligence* is one of uncovering all the potential surprises, revealing all the mysteries, and confirming all the information supplied to you by the seller. Most well-drafted offers provide the buyer with some period of time to conduct his or her due diligence. At the expiration, if the answers are not satisfactory, the buyer can cancel the contract and obtain a refund of the earnest money. This is not a normal part of a real estate contract form you purchase from an office supply store. If you require some time for due diligence, make sure the contract gives it to you.

How detailed should the due diligence clause be in a purchase contract?

Some commercial *purchase contracts* are very lengthy because they run on for pages about all the types of due diligence the buyer can conduct and the time limits for each category. If you are the seller, and the buyer is going to be able to tie up your property for six months while he or she thinks about things, he or she should just come out and say so. You, as the seller, know the buyer has thirty-two loopholes letting him or her cancel for any reason. Putting in a general due diligence clause with a six-month time limit makes more sense.

Besides a property inspection, what else do I need for due diligence?

At an absolute minimum, you should order a *title commitment* early in the investigation process. A title commitment will cost you a couple hundred dollars at the most. You can obtain a firm quote in advance. It gives you an early warning of any potential title problems. Some of them may take time to cure. Waiting until the day before closing, when you obtain a copy of the final title policy, is no time to start solving those problems. Also, the title commitment will let you know if all owners have signed your real estate contract. If the seller's spouse must sign any deed, did not sign the sales contract, and has no intention of signing any deed, it is best to find that out earlier rather than later.

You should always check the zoning on property by calling your local government zoning department. Just because a particular business is in operation at a location does not mean that same business can continue after a sale. The zoning might have changed over the years, with the current owner *grandfathered*. Changes in ownership could take away the grandfathering.

Even residential properties might suffer a change in zoning, if the area has gone commercial. In such an area, a house might have to be converted to business use, and no longer permitted residential occupancy.

In some states, sellers of residential properties are required to give you a disclosure form. Make sure you have it, read and understand it, and ask any follow-up questions. A disclosure regarding past water damage, for example, should prompt questions such as the following.

- How long ago was that?
- How did it happen?
- What did you do to make sure it will not happen again?
- How much did it cost to fix the problem?
- Did it take more than one attempt to fix the problem?
- What other problems did the water cause?
- Do you have a moisture bond for the property?
- What is the name and phone number of the person who did the repair work?
- Did he or she give you a written warranty?

Other than those aforementioned items, due diligence will depend on the particular property and your plans. If you plan to build something, you need to make sure the local government inspections department does not have any requirements that will make your project more expensive. Things like fire walls, sprinkler systems, particular types of lighting and wiring, changes in the placement of exit doors, and the numbers and widths of corridors can dramatically increase your expenses.

Talk to other property owners, and listen to their horror stories and near-misses. Read books, or cruise the Internet. There is always more to learn, no matter how experienced you become. For example, an engineer's compaction report shows how dense the dirt is on a site, and whether it will support the weight of a structure. However, the drilling for a compaction report generally goes down only six feet. Unscrupulous property owners sometimes fill deep holes with construction debris and tree stumps. The stumps will rot, the debris will settle, and the soil will become unstable. Only the top 6 or 7 feet is good, well-compacted clay or dirt, which is all the engineer tests—you get a clean report but a bad piece of property.

Documentary due diligence consists of reading all the leases in place for a property to make sure no one has any special deals. A tenant might be able to cancel his or her lease early with no penalty on a simple 60-days notice! He or she might have an option to buy the property—your property—for a set amount. Anything could be in those leases.

Most owners will not give you access to the actual tenants to obtain estoppel letters. An *estoppel letter* is the tenant's confirmation that his or her rent is a certain amount, his or her lease ends on a certain date, he or she has no claims or defenses against the landlord, and there are no side deals. As a result of your inability to obtain the estoppel letters, you will have to read every lease.

You will also need to see actual invoices for property bills to make sure they are as low as represented. For example, the owner of an office space might list marketing expenses of $2,000 per year. That figure was obtained by taking the combined advertising expense for all six of his or her properties—$12,000 per year—and dividing by six. Each property is charged its fair share of the overall expense. You may not be able to buy a phone directory or newspaper ad for only $2,000 per year. You should know that in advance.

How can I find due diligence checklists so I know what to check?

If you have access to a law library or Lexis/Nexis you might want to check a set of forms books called the *Transaction Guides*. This very useful set of books contains checklists for a wide variety of situations. They are intended to assist lawyers in representing their clients well and not overlooking important details. They are written in plain English and not too wordy, and I have found them to be very useful over the years.

Is securing my loan part of due diligence?

A well-written due diligence clause will let you cancel the contract without penalty if you find the deal is unworkable for any reason at all. That includes an inability to obtain acceptable financing terms. In that regard, getting your loan is part of due diligence, but that is the only reason. Financing is covered in the next section.

Chapter 21

CREDIT SCORES— BE THE MASTER OF YOUR CREDIT SCORE, NOT THE VICTIM OF IT

- What is a credit score?
- What information appears on my credit report?
- How do I find out my credit score?
- What is considered a good credit score?
- Will a poor credit score prevent me from obtaining a loan?
- Do other people besides lenders look at credit scores?
- How can I improve my credit score?
- I have heard that each time someone pulls a credit report, it lowers my score. Is that true?
- How do I correct my credit report?
- What credit information is too old and must be removed if you request it?
- I need my credit report corrected very quickly. Is that possible?

If you want to borrow money, you are going to be judged by your credit score. What is a credit score, who assigns it, and how can we improve it? These are all vital questions for any potential investor. Credit scores not only *determine* if you will be able to borrow money, but they also affect your interest rate, how much down payment will be required, and what your property insurance premiums will be.

What is a credit score?

Your *credit score* is a number assigned by one of the three major consumer credit-reporting agencies—Equifax, Experion, and TransUnion. It is also called a FICO score. This is short for the *Fair Isaac Company*, which wrote the software that calculates the score. (Recently, some large financial institutions have hired statistics specialists to design their own credit scoring software because they believe the national scores are not accurate for their regional differences, and they would like something more fine-tuned to evaluate loan requests.)

Just because the major credit reporting agencies all use the same software does not mean all three will have the same score for you. Most of your credit history and other information will be the same with all three of them; however, some will have more information than others. Those differences, and slight variations in their formulas, can make a difference in your score. That is why, when obtaining your credit score, you have to get it from each credit-reporting agency.

The score is supposed to be a numerical indicator of the likelihood you will pay your bills on time. It can be as low as 300 or as high as 850. The average score in the United States is around 723. According to the Fair Isaac Corporation website at **www.myfico.com**, this is what information goes into calculating a score:

Payment history:	35%
Amounts owed:	30%
Length of credit history:	15%
New credit:	10%
Types of credit used:	10%

What information appears on my credit report?

Not all of your credit history will appear on your credit report. As a result, many things might be good or bad about your credit history, but not affect your credit score.

As a general matter, the following will appear on your credit report:

- formal loans from banks and other financial institutions, finance companies, and auto company lenders;
- credit cards;
- lawsuits;
- accounts turned over to collection agencies;
- bankruptcies; and,
- tax liens.

Payments to utility companies, landlords, health care providers, or for business loans will normally not appear.

How do I find out my credit score?

By law, all three credit reporting agencies are required to give you one free credit report per year. In order to comply with the law, they set up a central phone number and website as a starting point. They are allowed to charge you for the actual credit score, but you can go to the same place as the credit reports to obtain it. The toll-free number is 877-322-8228 and the website is **www.annualcreditre-port.com**. Make a note of the website. The official site is *not*

www.freecreditreport.com, as most people think. That one is a commercial site that collects information and tries to sell a variety of services. You may or may not get your free credit report. Another excellent source is **www.myfico.com**, but it offers only the Equifax score, not the other two.

Note: The fee for your credit score is small—usually less than $15 each, and there are often promotions.

What is considered a good credit score?

Every lender has its own opinions regarding credit scores and how good or bad your score might be. As a very general matter, this is how they usually break down:

800 to 850	Perfect, or nearly perfect
750 to 799	Excellent
650 to 749	Very good
600 to 649	Fair
Below 600	Poor

Will a poor credit score prevent me from obtaining a loan?

There is usually someone out there willing to loan money to almost anyone. Generally speaking, the lower your credit score, the higher you can expect your interest rate to be. You may also have to pay a larger down payment. Also, you will have fewer choices of lenders and will have to work harder to find one willing to make a loan to you.

Substantial liquid assets (cash, stocks, and bonds) will almost always help a lender overlook your poor credit score. In addition, high-income individuals such as orthopedic surgeons and trial lawyers can usually explain away a poor credit score to the satisfaction of a lender. For most of us, though, we need to concentrate on improving that score if we want to borrow money.

Do other people besides lenders look at credit scores?

As a matter of fact, insurance companies use your credit score to see if you qualify for their best insurance rates. Their thinking is that people with problems managing credit also have more accidents and more insurable losses. You might disagree, but that is their pricing policy and you will not be able to convince them otherwise.

How can I improve my credit score?

Resist the urge to rush out and hire some company that promises to improve your credit score. Many of them employ illegal and unethical tactics that can get you in serious trouble. For the honest ones, you can do the same things yourself, and save the fee. Start working on your credit score six to twelve months before you want to borrow money. The time will pass fairly quickly, and you can shop for potential investments at the same time.

Below are some general guidelines for improving your score.

- Recent credit information has more weight than older information. Paying all your current bills on time each month is much more important than paying off old debts in their entirety.

- Paying off credit card balances completely will increase your score somewhat. Making large, but regular, reductions over time will result in dramatic increases. Credit scores test how well you pay your bills each month, not whether you do the right thing when you come into a large piece of cash.

- Do not obtain any new credit cards unless your low score is a result of insufficient credit. Even if you do not charge anything on them, simply having the cards can reduce your score.

- Changing jobs can reduce your score. If possible, stay with the job you have for awhile longer.

- Ask the credit reporting agency to delete incorrect or outdated information from your credit report.

I have heard that each time someone pulls a credit report, it lowers my score. Is that true?

There is some truth to that. If the credit reporting agency receives multiple requests for credit reports on you but no credit is granted shortly afterward, it assumes that you were turned down. Even with a good credit score, this might indicate that the local lenders know something about you that the credit reporting agency does not. Furthermore, multiple attempts to borrow money, without a loan resulting, seems to indicate a growing financial crisis.

On the other hand, your credit score does not take into account any reports granted within the prior thirty days. As a result, shopping for the best financing terms, shortly before receiving a loan, will not affect your score. In addition, several requests within a short time period, usually two weeks, indicate you are only shopping for the best deal. All of them will be counted as if there were only one request. If any of your existing creditors ask for updated reports for monitoring purposes, no matter how often, it does not decrease your score. Finally, you can obtain as many credit reports as you want on yourself. None of them will reduce your score.

How do I correct my credit report?

Federal consumer protection laws—the *Fair Credit Reporting Act*—require credit-reporting agencies to remove any incorrect or outdated information from their files on you.

If you give the agency a written protest regarding a specific item, they must check with whatever creditor reported the bad information about you. That creditor has thirty days to get back with the credit-reporting agency and either admit the mistake or confirm the information is accurate. If they admit the mistake, it is taken off immediately. If they do not answer at all within the thirty days, it is taken off immediately. If they confirm the information as accurate, then you will have to fight it with the creditor, not with the reporting agency.

This technicality—failure to confirm accuracy within thirty days—is what many unethical companies use to clean up their customers' credit reports. They tell their customers to protest everything. By the law of averages, some creditors will fail to answer on time, even though the information is accurate. This is highly unethical and it is illegal. Do not fall into that trap. It is far better to improve your score over time, the right way, than take shortcuts and possibly cause yourself more problems.

By law, information that is too old must be removed, even if it is accurate. It is sort of a statute of limitations on bad credit information. One exception is if you are applying for a loan of more than $150,000—in that instance, the old credit information can still be reported. As a practical matter, the credit reporting agencies do not disclose this information, even for larger loans.

What credit information is too old and must be removed if you request it?

- Civil suits, civil judgments, or arrest records older than ten years or the statute of limitations, whichever is longer.

- Paid tax liens older than seven years.

- Accounts placed for collection more than seven years ago. When in doubt, the Federal Trade Commission (which regulates compliance with the Fair Credit Reporting Act) assumes that an account will be placed for collection 180 days after it first becomes delinquent.

- Anything else, other than crimes, older than seven years.

Monitor your credit scores and credit reports three to four times a year in order to avoid nasty surprises.

I need my credit report corrected very quickly. Is that possible?

You can obtain what is called an *expedited handling* if you explain to the credit-reporting agency that you have a closing coming up in the next several days. Visit the official website below for links with telephone numbers:

www.annualcreditreport.com

Chapter 22

BORROWING MONEY

- I have a large mortgage on my home, car notes, and student loans. I will not qualify for additional debt. How can I invest in real estate?
- How much can I borrow?
- How much should I borrow?
- How do I find lenders for my property?
- What will I need to give a lender?
- What interest rate can I expect?
- Why are interest rates quoted in different ways?
- Can you explain the difference between face rate and annual percentage rate (APR)?
- How can I reduce my interest rate?
- Can I avoid personal liability for the loan?
- My accountant says I should have personal liability on the loan. Why is that?
- What are points?
- What do origination points cover?
- How do prepayment points work?
- Who will pay closing expenses associated with the purchase?
- Can I control my purchase closing expenses?
- How can I reduce loan closing expenses?
- Will my investment loan payments appear on my credit report?
- What information do I need to know about seller financing?

For most people, the ability to borrow money wisely—in sufficient amounts—is one of the critical keys to investing in real estate. There are several expressions related to this concept. One is "other people's money," (OPM), which refers to the idea that you should use borrowed funds, rather than your own cash, to increase the power of your investing dollars. The other common saying you will hear is about the "power of leverage." In physics, *leverage* is the ability to place a fulcrum at a certain point in order to increase your power. Think of a teeter-totter (or see-saw, depending on where you live). If you adjust the distance from the fulcrum, a small child on one end and a grown adult on the other can balance perfectly. In finance, borrowed money is the fulcrum. It lets you control a large investment, using a small amount of your own cash.

> **Example:** Suppose Amy and Mark want to buy real estate. Each inherits $100,000 and is willing to invest the entire amount. They decide to buy condos in a building near the college campus. The condos are selling for $100,000 each. They can be rented to students for $1,100 per month. Mark and Amy believe the values will increase by 50% in five years, at which time they will sell their investments.
>
> Amy wants as little risk as possible. She decides to buy one condo, and to pay cash. Mark is more adventurous. He will buy five condos, pay $20,000 down on each one, and borrow the remaining $80,000 for each unit. Let's assume he pays interest only, at 6%.
>
> This is what their financial picture looks like after five years:

	Amy	Mark
Cash invested	$100,000	$100,000
Units purchased	1	5
Debt	0	$400,000
Monthly rents	$1,100	$5,500
Monthly debt service	0	$2,000
Net monthly income	$1,100	$3,500
Total income over 5 yrs	$66,000	$210,000
Sales price	$150,000	$750,000
Sales profit	$50,000	$250,000
Profit + Income	**$116,000**	**$460,000**

That is the power of leverage.

I have a large mortgage on my home, car notes, and student loans. I will not qualify for additional debt. How can I invest in real estate?

Consumer lending is based on your personal income and the size of your other debts. A real estate investment stands on its own feet. If the anticipated income from the property will meet the mortgage payments, operating expense, plus a little extra for surprises, you will qualify for the loan.

If you wish to buy properties and flip them, you must have a realistic budget for necessary expenses until the resale and identify a source for the money to pay those expenses. If the money will come from borrowed funds—because you borrow enough to buy the property and to meet the expenses—then your personal lending credit limit does not matter. This concept is at the heart of private individuals' ability to invest in real estate.

How much can I borrow?

Experienced investors with a good track record or people with substantial liquid assets (cash, stock, and bonds) can often borrow 100% of the purchase price of property. Unless you are buying a fixer-upper or a personal residence, you will usually be able to borrow no more than a certain percentage of the purchase price of the property or the appraised value, *whichever is less*. That percentage can be 75% or 80%, depending on the lender and the property.

Here is an example of the "whichever is less" trap: You find a rental house with an appraised value of $100,000. Because the owner needs cash immediately, however, she is willing to sell it to you for only $75,000. If the lender has a 75% loan policy, you might think you can borrow the entire purchase price of $75,000 because it is 75% of the $100,000 appraised value. But, the lender will base its decision on 75% of the purchase price, giving you a loan of only $56,250.

How much should I borrow?

Generally, you should borrow the maximum amount possible within certain limitations.

- Do not borrow so much that it causes your loan to have a higher interest rate. Often, the less equity you have, the higher your interest rate will be.

- Think about the monthly mortgage payments and your ability to make them if your property is vacant. Try to borrow no more than what will result in mortgage payments you can meet for three or four months, even with no rental income.

How do I find lenders for my property?

For the beginning investor, the typical-size loan can be handled by the local branch of the financial institution that handles your checking or savings account. All lenders have differing rules for the size transaction loan officers can handle. These are called *delegations of authority*. A branch manager might have authority to make a loan up to $75,000, the citywide commercial loan officer might have authority to make a loan up to $250,000, and all loans over that might need approval from the regional office.

Be sure to visit your own financial institution, and three or four others that have good reputations. Ask each of them, point-blank, "What are the approval limits for different sizes of loans?" It is always surprising to people, but a beginning investor, with a good reputation among the local population, might find it easier to borrow money from a different bank. That is because the other bank might have local loan approval authority, while the investor's bank might need to obtain approval from a regional office.

What will I need to give a lender?

Most lenders require your personal financial statement showing your assets (bank accounts, stocks and bonds, whole-life insurance policies, house, autos, etc.) and liabilities (loans, credit cards, unpaid taxes, etc.) They will also need a *cash flow statement*, showing your average monthly income, and where the money goes each month. A lender wants to know that you are not living paycheck to paycheck, and can afford to make mortgage payments even if the property is vacant for a few months. It is all right to have no surplus cash at the end of each month, but you will need some money in savings or in liquid assets in order to make up for it.

You will also need a letter or a *fact sheet* stating the purchase price of the property, anticipated closing expenses, and your investment intentions, such as buy and rent out, buy and sell relatively soon, or buy and hold for future sale.

For rental income property, you will need to show anticipated annual income and expenses for the property. Property planned for resale should state the purchase price you expect to receive, what evidence you have that it is a reasonable expectation (for example, comparable sales in the area), and the expenses you will have holding and then selling the property.

Photos of the property, a map with the location marked, and a general description of the area will always help. If it will be used for residential rental, include a statement regarding all school zones for the property. That way, the lender can easily evaluate that the property is in a good area and will hold its value.

If you plan to manage the property yourself, say so in your documents and explain any relevant experience. A carpenter husband and his plumber wife have more property management credibility than a surgeon husband and his lawyer wife, for example. On the other hand, the surgeon/lawyer team can probably afford to hire maintenance and management from third parties.

Finally, if this is the just the beginning of your investment career, with more purchases (and more loans) to follow, then say so. Lenders are more willing to invest in a first-time real estate investor if they believe that other business will follow.

> **Tip:** Always put everything in writing. Lenders talk to lots of people. Conversations can get mixed up many times. Putting things in writing can prevent potentially disastrous misunderstandings that could result in your loan request being turned down.

What interest rate can I expect?

You are probably most familiar with *home loan* interest rates, because those are the ones most often advertised in the newspapers and on television. Home loans are almost always at lower rates than investment loans, usually by one-half to one percentage point. If you qualify for a 6.5% loan to buy a home as a residence, you will probably have to pay 7% interest to buy that same home to use as a rental house.

Why are interest rates quoted in different ways?

Lenders have differing methods of arriving at the interest rate they will charge for loans. Many start with a reference point, which is called the *index*. Next, they tell you that your loan will be a certain amount above whatever the index is on the relevant day. That day could be the date of the *quote* (very rare), the date of a *firm loan commitment* (more common), or the date of the *loan closing* (very common.) For example, a lender might agree to loan you $80,000 on a 25-year mortgage at 135 basis points over the 10-year treasury bond rate. If 10-year treasuries are at 5.2% on the date of the commitment or the date of the loan, then your interest rate will be 5.2% + 1.35%, or 6.55%.

Other lenders will quote you a particular interest rate, which they will honor for a limited period of time. If that time expires before you are ready to close, you will have to shop for new rates with everyone all over again. This can be very inefficient.

Can you explain the difference between face rate and annual percentage rate (APR)?

The *face rate* for a loan is the amount that will appear on your promissory note. It does not take into account additional borrowing costs and certain lender-required fees and expenses. Suppose you borrowed $100 for one year and paid $106 at the end of the year. Your interest rate is 6%—that is pretty easy. What if, instead, you had to pay a $10 fee for the lender to evaluate your loan request and fill out some paperwork? In that case, the loan cost you $10 in advance, and $6 at the end. The real cost of that loan is much greater than 6%. That is what the APR calculation attempts to reveal to you.

If First National Bank will charge you 7.5% interest with no closing costs or loan fees, that might be cheaper, overall, than Last State Bank, which quotes you 7% interest but with thousands of dollars in loan fees that must either be paid at closing or included in your loan. The mechanism that allows you to compare your options in this situation is something called the *annual percentage rate* (APR). You should ask all potential lenders for their estimate of the APR on your loan, and an itemized list of loan fees and expenses you can reasonably expect, with an estimate of the amount.

How can I reduce my interest rate?

Aside from competitive shopping, several things will reduce your interest rate among almost all lenders. The following are some general rules of thumb.

- The larger your equity in the property, the lower your interest rate will be, because the lender has a smaller risk of loss due to foreclosure.

- A loan with monthly principal and interest payments will have a lower interest rate than one that calls for interest payments only, with the principal due some time in the future.

- Better credit scores qualify you for cheaper interest rates. Even if your credit score is good enough to obtain a loan, see if improving it might reduce your rate.

- The shorter the loan term, the lower you can expect your interest rate to be. Generally speaking, a 15-year mortgage will have lower rates than a 30-year or 50-year mortgage.

- Some lenders will give you a cheaper rate if you already have other loans with them or agree to place your checking account with them. Be aware, however, that some lenders will require you to keep your property operating account with them as a condition of the loan. This is so they can keep track of the money in the account and have a possible early warning if you are headed into financial trouble.

- Paying loan points (different from origination points) will allow you to "buy down" your interest rate. For example, a lender might say, "You qualify for 8.25% interest. But, you can pay a fee equal to 2% of the loan, and we can reduce your rate to 8%."

Can I avoid personal liability for the loan?

Most lenders will require beginning investors to sign the mortgage loan with full personal liability in case there is a default. If you are buying property in the name of a corporation or similar entity and the loan is in the same name, the lender will usually ask you to guarantee the loan.

The lender wants to know that you have some "skin in the game." In other words, the lender wants you just as worried as he or she is in regard to paying the mortgage on time every month. If you have nothing at risk except the loss of your down payment, you might decide to walk away and let the lender foreclose if there are problems.

If you are a financially strong borrower with an excellent reputation, or if you are experienced and known to your lender, you can avoid personal liability in two ways. One is by borrowing the money in a corporate name and not guaranteeing the note. If the corporation has only one asset—the property you bought—then the most you will lose in a financial disaster is the property. The lender will not be able to sue you in case foreclosure does not pay off the loan completely. The other method is to tell the lender that you want the loan to be *non-recourse,* or a *dry mortgage.* The documents will need to specify that you will have no personal liability in the event of default.

Surprisingly, it is much easier to obtain non-recourse financing with larger loans—those in excess of $3 million. It is also much easier to obtain 100% development financing for larger loans. It is something to think about as you become more confident in your investing skills.

My accountant says I should have personal liability on the loan. Why is that?

Something in the tax law called the *at risk rules* limits the amount of your tax deductions depending on how much money you have at risk in the investment. The IRS will not allow you to deduct investment property expenses against other income (such as your salary or wages) unless you have equity in the property or you are personally liable for the financing. Read more about this subject in Chapter 31.

What are points?

Points are confusing because there are two different kinds. Both kinds are calculated by starting with the amount of your loan. One point equals 1% of your loan. A quote of "three points" for a $100,000 loan means the points will be 3% of $100,000, or $3,000.

That is fairly simple. It gets complicated when you want to know what the points are for. One kind, called *origination points,* is a lender fee to cover certain expenses and additional profit for the lender. On a typical commercial loan, the origination points will be 0.5%–1% of the loan. This is very negotiable, but most lenders will not waive it entirely.

The other kind of points is a *prepaid interest*, used to *buy down* your interest rate on the loan, which means reducing it below the typical quoted rate. This is entirely at your option. The lender cannot force you to pay this kind of points.

What do origination points cover?

Lenders all include different expenses within their origination points. There is no rule regarding what is covered. One might charge you 0.5% of the loan, but you will also have to pay for the lender's attorney's fees, appraisal, and survey. Another might charge 1% of the loan, but with no additional expenses. You cannot compare the loans until you know what your additional expenses will be. That is why you always have to ask each lender every time, even if you use the same lender for several different loans. Policies can change while you are not looking!

How do prepayment points work?

Prepayment points, usually simply called "points," are a fee you pay in order to obtain a reduced interest rate. In effect, you are paying some of your interest in advance, so the lender is willing to make your loan at a lower rate.

> **Example:** Suppose you are willing to loan $100 to your brother for one year at 10% simple interest. At the end of one year, your brother will pay you $110. Suppose, instead, you said, "Brother, if you pay five points, I will reduce my interest rate to 5%." This means you will loan your brother $100, but at exactly the same time, he will pay you $5 (5% of the loan amount). As a practical matter, all your brother receives from the transaction is a net

gain of $95. At the end of one year, he will pay you the loan amount, plus 5% interest, for a total of $105. He is still out $110, total, and you still receive $110, total, *but* you receive $5 a whole year earlier than you would have otherwise.

You can see from this example how prepayment points can be a good thing for the lender, as well as a bad thing for the borrower. By making your brother pay five points in exchange for reducing the interest rate on the $100 loan, you can take the $5 he pays up front, put it in a bank, and earn interest on it for a whole year. Your brother, on the other hand, had to take that $5 out of the bank in order to pay you when the loan was made, which means he also loses the interest he was earning on it.

To make matters more complicated, suppose your brother found a $100 bill in an old trousers pocket and decided to repay his loan to you after only six months. You received $5 when the loan was made. That is your money to keep, no matter what. At the end of six months, your brother will owe one half year's interest on $100 at 5% interest, or $2.50. He will pay you $102.50. So, you receive a total of $7.50 for a six-month loan on $100. That is an annual interest rate of 15%, without even taking into account the benefit of getting $5 of the money up front. This is a good example of why prepayment points rarely make sense for people who will keep their loans for five years or less. The numbers just do not work out very well for the borrower.

The exception is when the seller pays the points for you. This is not uncommon. If the seller pays the points, then it probably makes no difference to you. Why would a seller pay your points, instead of just reducing the sales price? Remember, lenders will loan you a percentage of the sales price or the appraised value, whichever is less. If the seller reduces his or her sales price, that also reduces your loan amount. You might be willing to have a higher sales price with a larger loan, but at a lower interest rate. Refer to Appendix C for more information on running real estate numbers.

Who will pay closing expenses associated with the purchase?

Remember, closing expenses fall into two categories. The first is *purchase* closing expenses, which are the expenses you would have even if you paid cash for the property. The second is *loan* closing expenses, which are the expenses directly connected to your loan.

Deciding who will pay purchase closing expenses is entirely a matter of negotiation between the seller and the buyer. There is no law or rule regarding who has to pay what. Many real estate agents will advise you, "The buyer pays the deed recording fee, because the seller does not care if you ever record it or not. It makes no difference to him or her." This might be true, but it does not mean you are prevented from negotiating the seller's agreement that he or she will pay the recording fees. A motivated seller afraid of losing a sale might agree to pay all purchase closing expenses. A seller in a hot market might not agree to pay any of them.

Normally, the borrower pays all loan closing expenses, but that is also a matter of negotiation between buyer and seller.

Can I control my purchase closing expenses?

Most purchase closing expenses are fairly cut and dried with no room for negotiation or shopping. The title insurance is what it is. Recording fees are set by law. Document preparation fees are pretty standardized.

Waiting until the last minute to clear up problems can rack up a lot of expenses in overnight delivery and courier charges and long-distance calls. Not only is it stressful, it is also expensive. Try to avoid it. Wire transfer fees generally add a small cost, but I do not recommend mailing certified checks in order to avoid the wire transfer fee. First, overnight delivery fees are about the same as wire transfer fees. Second, you do not really want to drop that check in the mail with just a regular stamp, do you? Third, even cashier's checks can have holds placed on them because of widespread fraud and the little known ability to stop payment on a cashier's check. Wired funds are instant.

The best control is to negotiate that the other party pays the closing expenses. A motivated seller will agree to pay all of them.

How can I reduce loan closing expenses?

Ask each potential lender for an itemized list of the types of loan closing expenses you can expect, and an estimate of the amount. Typical sources of unexpectedly large fees include the following.

- *Attorney's fees.* Unless your lender is willing to commit to a *not-to-exceed number*, called a *cap*, these can stack up in a hurry. If a lawyer charges $300 per hour, with a quarter-hour minimum time entry, then three rounds of telephone tag ending in a simple conversation with the loan officer consisting of, "Have you received proof of insurance yet?" can add up to $525 in fees! Every time you ask a question about the documents or requirements, every time the lawyer talks to anyone or has to review the file, the meter is running.

- *Title insurance.* There is the standard, simple title insurance policy, and then there are additional things called endorsements that provide extra coverage for the lender. Each endorsement costs you more money. Lenders all have different requirements regarding which endorsements they want. They might be willing to waive some of them.

- *Surveys.* Again, all lenders have different amounts of information they want to see on a survey. The more information the surveyor has to include, the more expensive the survey will be. Some lenders are happy with a drawing that shows property lines and a statement that all buildings are inside the property lines. Others want every single structure, all fences, driveways, sidewalks, storm sewers, and power line easements marked on the drawing. You can control this expense in three ways: (1) obtain a cap, just like with legal fees; (2) find out what the specific survey requirements are, and whether a lender with a larger interest rate might end up being cheaper because its closing expenses are cheaper; and, (3) see if the seller already has a survey that can be updated fairly cheaply.

- *Phase I Environmental Report.* This is an engineer's report to the lender that, based on the history of the property and interviews with knowledgeable people, there is no evidence that the property might contain hazardous waste. There is a wide range of fees among engineers for these services, so you should ask for the ability to choose the cheapest engineer who is on the lender's approved list.

Will my investment loan payments appear on my credit report?

Normally, the payment history on an investment loan will not appear on your credit report. Such loans are usually booked as commercial loans. Consumer credit information appears on consumer credit reports. There may be exceptions. Face it, sometimes you might be forced to decide which loan to pay a little bit late now and then. You may need to know how that decision will affect your credit score. Find out early who reports and who does not, and make your decisions accordingly.

What information do I need to know about seller financing?

There are many other considerations when thinking about seller financing. That topic is covered in the next chapter.

Chapter 23

SELLER FINANCING—AN IMPORTANT SOURCE OF MONEY

- How much seller financing can I receive?
- What is a wraparound mortgage?
- Even if I cannot find an assumable loan, should I do a wraparound mortgage?
- I know that some loans do not have due-on-sale clauses. Should I consider a wrap in those situations?
- Why would a seller hold financing?
- I am embarrassed to ask about seller financing because I am worried the seller will think I cannot qualify for a loan. Is this common?
- What things need to be negotiated for seller financing?
- Can I negotiate the terms of seller financing after the sales contract is signed?
- I cannot buy anything unless I am able to get seller financing. What is the best way to find these sellers?
- If I, as an investor, sell property and hold the financing, what should I be aware of?

A surprising number of property sellers would be willing to finance your purchase, if only someone explained the advantages to them. As you build your real estate portfolio and begin selling off properties, you might also find *seller financing* an attractive option. There are two major types.

- Basic seller financing, just like mortgage company financing.

- Variations on the lease option, in which the seller retains title to the property and the buyer receives a deed only after all the payments have been made. In states with poor consumer protection laws, one missed payment could result in complete forfeiture of all money previously paid and loss of the right to cure the default and eventually receive a deed.

How much seller financing can I receive?

Pretty much anything is possible with seller financing. Someone who owns his or her property free and clear does not need any sale proceeds to pay off his or her mortgage. He or she might be willing to give you 100% financing. Others might want a down payment in some percentage, just like a bank or mortgage company. Many times a seller will agree to hold a second mortgage on the property for a short period of time. You also obtain regular mortgage money. Instead of making a down payment for the balance due to the seller, you make monthly payments for three to five years to the seller. At the end, you refinance everything with a traditional lender and pay off the seller.

What is a wraparound mortgage?

Wraparound mortgages used to be very common nationwide up until the mid 1980s. Today they are rare, but not entirely extinct. A *wraparound mortgage* is best understood by an example.

> **Example:** Tyler buys a $150,000 home by paying $30,000 down and financing the balance with a mortgage loan from Friendly Mortgage Company. The loan is at a fixed interest rate of 5% per year. On a 30-year loan, his payments are $644.19 per month.
>
> Ten years later, Tyler wants to sell his home to Carson for $300,000. Carson either cannot borrow the money, or perhaps interest rates have increased to 10% and he does not want to pay such a high rate. Tyler says to Carson, "I will give you a deed to the house. Pay me $30,000 as a down payment. Then, we can do a wraparound mortgage for the remaining $270,000, at a very cheap 8% interest. In other words, we will "wrap" our new mortgage around my old mortgage. We will not tell the lender we are doing this. You will make payments to me of $1,981.16 per month. Out of that, I will make my first mortgage payments of $644.19 per month and keep the rest. The mortgage will continue to be in my name."

This example works only if Tyler's loan is assumable—if his lender does not have something called a *due on sale clause* in its mortgage. The clause says that, if the property is sold, the loan balance must be paid in full at the time of sale. Virtually every mortgage loan made since the mid 1980s has such a clause, making it almost impossible to do a "wrap." There are some limited exceptions to the enforceability of the clause. Transfers to a spouse or children because of divorce or to an heir because of death will not cause the mortgage balance to be due.

Even if I cannot find an assumable loan, should I do a wraparound mortgage?

Some gurus will tell you it is okay if you do not tell the lender about the sale. They say that a technical reading of the documents shows that no one has any obligation to tell the lender when property is sold. Some say that if you disguise the transaction as a lease or a lease-option, you can avoid the due on sale clause. Others disagree, saying that if the substance of the transaction is a sale, then the first mortgage must be paid in full at the time of the sale. I think that any buyer or seller who does a wrap when the first mortgage has a due on sale clause is asking for trouble. Approach this type of seller financing with caution.

I know that some loans do not have due-on-sale clauses. Should I consider a wrap in those situations?

A big problem with wraparound mortgages is caused by the possibility of bad tax consequences to both parties. The rule is pretty technical, there are loopholes, and there are landmines inside some things that look like loopholes. Beware!

In a nutshell, sellers may have to declare all gain as income in the year of the sale and pay income taxes, instead of spreading it out over the lifetime of the wrap as they receive their money. Buyers may not be able to deduct wraparound mortgage interest payments on their taxes. Seek professional advice before doing a wrap, and be sure to ask your advisor about these specific issues. Many attorneys and accountants are not aware of the potential problems.

Why would a seller hold financing?

Sellers agree to hold financing because it is economically beneficial for them. Keep this thought always in mind. You will not be bashful about asking for seller financing and you will not be scared to offer seller financing on your own sales because you will know it is a win-

win situation.

Some sellers cannot afford to be your lender. If a seller needs the equity in his or her home in order to finance the purchase of another home, then he or she is not going to be a prospect for you.

For the rest, remember that a seller who receives a large chunk of cash has a problem. He or she must find a safe investment for that money with attractive earnings. Bank certificates of deposit are very safe but earn very low interest rates. The stock market might be much better but has much higher risk. Many sellers would be eager to earn the same interest rate as mortgage lenders, or even a little bit less. They already know the property they are selling to you and are confident it will hold its value as collateral.

It is quirky, but many sellers will hold the financing if you will agree to their above-market price for the property. You might not care about the higher price if your money can work out the same.

	Bank financing	Seller financing
Purchase price	$120,000	$135,000
Down payment	$24,000	$0
Interest rate	7%	5%
Loan term	30 years	30 years
Monthly payment	$638.69	$724.71
Total payments	$229,928	$260,895
Total interest	$133,928	$125,895
Total payments, including down payment	$253,928	$260,895
Difference in total payments	-$6,967	+$6,967

Below is a chart comparing seller financing and bank financing on a property, if the seller wanted a higher price but would be your lender at a lower interest rate.

Paying the seller's $15,000 higher price actually costs you only

$6,967 over the course of thirty years. Plus, you do not have to make a down payment. If you had $24,000 to use for a down payment, you could use it for a second investment instead.

As always, when evaluating an opportunity, be sure to run the numbers, and see Appendix C if you have any difficulties. Things that might seem good or bad at first glance might turn out to be quite different after a little scrutiny.

I am embarrassed to ask about seller financing because I am worried the seller will think I cannot qualify for a loan. Is this common?

It is very common for buyers to be hesitant about asking for seller financing. Many of them think exactly the same thing—asking the question makes it look like they are not credit worthy. This is not the case. Many very wealthy and sophisticated investors try to obtain seller financing whenever possible.

When bringing up the subject, the direct approach is usually best. You could say, "If available, I always prefer seller financing because it is such a win-win situation. I pay interest rates a little below what traditional lenders charge, you receive interest rates a good bit higher than banks pay on certificates of deposit and a lot safer than the stock market. Is this something we can explore on this deal?" If the property is the seller's residence, he or she probably qualifies for the $250,000 worth of gain ($500,000 for married couples) as tax-free under current tax laws. If it is not his or her personal residence, however, you might also say, "You know, if you hold the financing, you can spread your taxes out over many years, instead of paying them all this year. Would that be attractive to you?"

What things need to be negotiated for seller financing?

The following is a list of things you should agree upon with the seller. I like to attach this list to a real estate offer as an addendum. For some reason, most people do not read pre-printed contracts. They read only the information in the blanks. But, if you attach something else, like an addendum, they will read the entire addendum but might reject the offer if it is not easy to understand, so keep it simple.

1. How much of the purchase price will be financed by the seller?
2. What will the annual interest rate be?
3. Will the interest rate change from time to time?
4. If the interest rate will change, how often will it change?
5. If the interest will change, how will the new interest rate be calculated each time?
6. How long will you hold the financing, until the entire balance will be due in full if not paid off earlier?
7. How will the monthly payments be calculated? (examples: interest only, principal and interest calculated as if the loan were a 15-, 20-, 25-, 30-, 40-, or 50-year (pick one) fully amortizing loan)
8. If I sell the property, will the new owner be allowed to assume the loan?

Can I negotiate the terms of seller financing after the sales contract is signed?

In most states, the above terms of seller financing must be included in the real estate sales contract. Otherwise, the seller might be able to agree to seller financing in the sales contract and later change his or her mind. Most courts will hold that, because the parties did not spell out important terms of their financing arrangements, the financing portion of the agreement is not enforceable at all.

I cannot buy anything unless I am able to get seller financing. What is the best way to find these sellers?

There are several ways to find sellers highly likely to hold the financing for you.

Every community has a few people who specialize in buying investment properties and then selling them and holding the financing through a vehicle called a *bond for title, land sale contract, contract for deed,* or *lease option contract.* Those people are generally well known in the community because of the large volume of their real estate transactions. Ask a few real estate agents, escrow companies, or real estate lenders for some names.

> **Note:** This is a very risky form of seller financing, so be careful. You do not receive a deed until every payment has been made in full. Some states have very poor consumer protection laws in this area. If you make payments for ten years and then miss one payment, you could lose the property and all the equity you thought you were building up. Other states treat these transactions as if they were mortgage loans, and give buyers protections regarding notice of default, opportunity to cure the default, and other such issues. Be sure to find out the laws in your state before pursuing this course.

Senior citizens are more likely to hold the financing than younger people. That is because a senior citizen who has held property for a long period of time probably has little or no debt on it. If the property is a home, it may have no mortgage debt, even if it was a relatively recent purchase. If the seller does not need cash from you to pay off his or her mortgage, and he or she does not need cash from you to buy another property, then the seller is a good prospect to hold the financing. Seniors are excellent prospects because they will usually owe no taxes upon the sale of their home, especially when buying homes to use as rentals. They do not need cash at closing.

Current investors selling their rental properties are good seller financing possibilities. Just because they are selling does not mean the property is a bad investment. The current owner might be trading up to something larger, consolidating into certain neighborhoods, or simply tired of dealing with tenants. The owner is, however, used to regular monthly income from his or her properties. He or she is also aware of the continuing value of the property as collateral. Selling the property and holding a mortgage on it makes perfect sense for such people.

Finally, you might want to make it a habit to ask about seller financing right at the beginning of any discussion. There is no point wasting time learning about all the features of property and viewing it if you cannot buy it. Begin each conversation with, "I limit my investments to those with seller financing because I find it is such a win-win situation for both parties. Is that available for this property?"

If I, as an investor, sell property and hold the financing, what should I be aware of?

You should do most of the things a regular lender does to protect his or her interests, which include the following.

- Pay for a lawyer to draft the note, mortgage, and any related documents for you. Taking forms off the Internet or from a book can be risky if you do not fully understand all the verbiage. If at all possible, ask your lawyer to use the standard Federal National Mortgage Association or Federal Home Loan Mortgage

Corporation for your state. That way, if you later want to cash out and sell the note and mortgage in the nationwide marketplace called the *secondary market*, that will be easy to do.

- Make sure everything is prepared just as if you were doing business with strangers, especially when dealing with friends and relatives. This helps you avoid misunderstandings. Plus, you never know what is going to happen with that relationship later. It might fall apart, especially if there are money problems.

- Require proof of property insurance that protects your interest. Make sure you are listed as an additional insured on the policy. Read Chapter 29 for details regarding the best kinds of insurance.

Note: Currently, I could find no company willing to write PMI insurance (see Chapter 29) for individuals. Be very careful before you agree to hold financing greater than 80% of the value of your property.

Chapter 24

CLOSING— WHAT HAPPENS AT CLOSING

- Who chooses the closing company?
- I would like to obtain copies of closing documents before closing so I have time to read them. Is that possible?
- How does the closing company know how to split up the expenses?
- What is title insurance?
- Why do I need an owner's policy in addition to the required lender's policy?
- Besides the deed and loan documents, what other documents need to be signed at closing?
- What is the FIRPTA affidavit?
- Will I receive a settlement statement?
- Who records my deed?

Closing is the event when all documents are signed and delivered, and all money changes hands.

Who chooses the closing company?

As a practical matter, the real estate agent representing the buyer usually recommends a closing company and everyone goes along with that. The closing company must be approved by the buyer's lender, and the title insurance company must also be approved. Make sure these two choices are on the approved list before proceeding too far down the road.

Under the federal *Real Estate Settlement and Procedures Act* (RESPA), it is illegal for a seller to require a particular closing company. The seller can merely recommend someone, and the buyer may or may not agree.

I would like to obtain copies of closing documents before closing so I have time to read them. Is that possible?

Even in a law firm, real estate closings are generally prepared by a team of secretaries, legal assistants, and paralegals. Almost every single scrap of paper is a form that comes off the computer. Do not be bashful about asking for copies of the forms ahead of time, with blank spaces instead of your particular information. That way you can read them and ask questions instead of feeling pressured to simply sign your name without reading anything.

Loan documents usually arrive only a day or two before closing. Your lender will have a checklist of its requirements and some standard forms. Ask for copies.

How does the closing company know how to split up the expenses?

If a real estate agent is involved, he or she will normally deliver a copy of the purchase contract to the closing company. If the parties do not have an agent, then the buyer normally delivers all documents to the closing company.

What is title insurance?

Title insurance is a policy that protects the lender, the buyer, or both if title defects arise after closing. The policy might pay off someone with a competing claim, or it might pay all legal expenses to contest someone else's claim.

This might happen in a thousand different ways, but here is one common example.

> **Example:** Lorenzo agrees to sell you a piece of property for $100,000. You go to closing and pay him his money. Three months later, the IRS reveals it had a recorded tax lien against Lorenzo for $75,000. It recorded its lien one hour before closing, which means that your property is now subject to that lien. The IRS wants $75,000 from you, or it is going to foreclose its lien and take your property. Title insurance will pay off the IRS, and then the title insurance company will track down Lorenzo to reiumburse it.

Why do I need an owner's policy in addition to the required lender's policy?

Suppose you buy a rental house from John, who says he is the owner. You pay $100,000, of which $80,000 came from Last National Bank. There is a lender's title policy, but you never purchased an owner's title policy.

One month later, Rafe, John's brother and the real owner of the rental house, shows up after a tour of military duty overseas. He claims his brother impersonated him and forged his signature. Rafe does not want to sell his house for any price. The title insurance company cannot pay off Rafe, and it cannot fight him. Instead, it will pay policy limits—$80,000—on the title insurance. Last National Bank will receive $80,000 under its lender's policy.

However, because you do not have an owner's title policy, you will receive nothing. You will not owe any money under the original loan—this is what the title insurance company took care of when it paid Last National Bank—but you also will not have your $20,000 down payment anymore. You are out of luck! If you had an owner's title policy, you would be entitled to your $20,000 back from the title company. That is why you always obtain an owner's policy.

Besides the deed and loan documents, what other documents need to be signed at closing?

In his or her research regarding the title, the lawyer might discover judgments or liens against people with names similar to yours or the seller's. If that happens, the lawyer may require proof that you are not the person with the judgment or lien. He or she will usually also require *name affidavits*, in which you state, under oath, that you are a different person than the one who has a lien against him or her.

Most states allow repair or construction people to file liens against property for unpaid services. As a result, the closing attorney will ask the seller to sign forms saying that there have not been any repairs within the last six months or so (depending on your state's time limits), or that all repairs have been paid in full.

You, as the buyer, will have to sign a lot of forms agreeing that everything possible has been disclosed to you, you have read every single page of every single document, and you have no unanswered questions.

What is the FIRPTA affidavit?

FIRPTA is short for *Foreign Investment in Real Property Tax Act*. Congress was concerned that foreign sellers would sell their property and then not pay any income taxes on the sale proceeds. As a result, it required that buyers withhold 10% of the purchase price and pay it over to the IRS. The seller could then apply to the IRS for a refund, if one was due. This caused an incredible number of headaches, however, so the IRS allowed a huge loophole. If the buyer signs an affidavit saying the purchase price is less than $300,000 *or* the buyer currently has steadfast plans to live in the property at least 50% of the time, then no one has to fool with the IRS withholding issues.

Will I receive a settlement statement?

The *settlement statement* shows all money paid at closing and how it was disbursed. It itemizes all credits and all debits for both the buyer and the seller. For home purchases, the form that is used is specified by federal law. It is called a HUD-1. Because all closing software works well with the HUD-1 form, most closing companies use it even for commercial loans.

The HUD-1 form is printed on legal-sized paper with small print. It is virtually impossible to reproduce in this book in any meaningful manner. You can find samples on the Internet, such as on the website of the U.S. Department of Housing and Urban Development, at **www.hud.gov/offices/hsg/sfh/res/resappa.cfm**. It includes links to and instructions for completing a sample form.

Note: If you are interested in having a template so you can estimate your own closing costs, many companies sell software and templates for a very reasonable price. Do an Internet search on "HUD-1 software," and you will find prices from hundreds of dollars to free downloads. Obviously, the more expensive packages will take care of a wider variety of transactions. You will just have to look at what everyone has to offer, and decide which is best for you.

Who records my deed?

The title company or closing attorney will almost always record your deed for you. That is because they are writing the title insurance, and it is in their best interests to make sure your deed gets recorded before any possible judgment or lien against the seller.

Chapter 25

CLOSING COSTS— CONTROL CLOSING EXPENSES

- What are closing costs, exactly?
- What are the most common types of closing costs?
- The seller already has title insurance. Can we use the same policy?
- Can other expenses be reduced if we use existing work?
- Who pays which closing costs?
- How can I estimate my own closing costs?
- What happens after closing?

Of all the surprises that can occur when investing in real estate, closing costs are most often overlooked. If you have limited cash, spending too much in closing costs could mean you have too little for rehab expenses, too much pressure to put any tenant in place rather than waiting for a good one, and any number of other problems. Avoid all of them by being able to estimate your own closing costs.

What are closing costs, exactly?

Closing costs, sometimes called *settlement costs*, consist of all the expenses associated with transferring title to real estate, recording deeds and other documents, dividing ongoing income and expenses fairly between buyer and seller, complying with government paperwork, and all the other services regarding the protection of buyers and lenders in the transaction.

Although they are not technically closing costs, many lenders have fees and expenses that must be paid in advance before they will even consider your loan request. Also, bear in mind that certain items of *due diligence*—making sure the property is suitable for your needs—will have their own associated expenses. Read Chapter 20 on due diligence for details, but remember to factor those expenses into your budget as well.

What are the most common types of closing costs?

- Document preparation
- Title inspection
- Recording fees
- Closing agent fees
- Survey
- Inspections
- Prepaid insurance
- Attorney's fees
- Title insurance
- Transfer taxes and fees
- Real estate agent fees
- Appraisal
- Loan fees
- Prorated expenses

The Department of Housing and Urban Development (HUD) has a *Settlement Cost Booklet* on its website at **www.hud.gov/offices/hsg/ sfh/res/sfhrestc.cfm**. It includes a calculator for estimating your closing costs.

If you are investing in single-family homes or small (quadraplexes or smaller) apartments, you can expect your closing costs to be fairly consistent with buying a home in the same price range. There are examples in the HUD online booklet that should help you a lot.

> **Tip:** Larger commercial loans may have more lender fees. When shopping for financing, you should ask for disclosure of all loan-related fees, including those that must be paid before the loan is approved and those that will be paid at closing.

The largest uncontrolled expense for commercial loans is attorney's fees. Ask the lender to give you a *not-to-exceed figure*, so that any fees in excess of that number will be paid by the lender. If that is not possible, request an estimate and some advice regarding how you can minimize those expenses. Most commercial lenders will be happy to give you a copy of their standard closing checklist. A meeting with the lender and attorneys to determine who will perform what items on the checklist could save you hundreds or even thousands of dollars in fees.

Before the attorneys get involved, however, find out your lender's standard title insurance endorsement requirements. Every additional coverage added to the title insurance policy costs you more money.

Investment properties that already generate rental income, such as apartments or office buildings, will have some additional items accounted for at closing. Depending on the date of the month, some portion of the rental income already paid to the seller will actually belong to you. That amount will need to be prorated, and you will receive a credit against your purchase price for the amounts collected by the seller. Some prepaid expenses, such as insurance premiums, will be partially your responsibility for your period of ownership. The seller will receive a credit for those items. By contract, tenant security deposits will become your obligation to reimburse at the end of their term. The seller will either transfer its deposit escrow account to you, or will give you a credit for those deposits, depending on state law and local custom.

The seller already has title insurance. Can we use the same policy?

Each transaction requires a new title insurance policy. You can, however, often obtain a discount called a *reissue credit*. Some companies will give the credit only if they wrote the prior policy. Some will recognize competitors' title policies and give you the discount, but you will need to give them a copy of the earlier policy. Usually there is a five-year time limit—anything older than that will not qualify for a discount.

Can other expenses be reduced if we use existing work?

Often, a surveyor will charge a small fee to update a survey previously prepared by him or her. Surveys prepared by others do not normally enjoy the same courtesy.

Appraisals are always prepared fresh, for each transaction, as are any required engineering reports.

Who pays which closing costs?

There is no rule regarding who pays which closing costs. This is absolutely a matter of negotiation between buyer and seller. It is not uncommon for one or the other to pay all the closing costs. It depends on who is the more motivated person, and who is the better negotiator.

Typically, the seller will pay for the owner's title policy, deed preparation, and transfer taxes. The buyer will pay for all loan-related fees and recording fees. The parties will split the closing company fees. There is nothing sacred about this custom, however.

How can I estimate my own closing costs?

If a real estate agent is involved in the transaction, he or she can usually give you an estimate of the closing costs except for those related to your loan. In many states, real estate agents are required to give that information to their clients and customers.

For consumer loans, the lender is required to give you an estimate of the closing expenses. This is not a requirement for business loans, but you can still ask for and receive the same information.

Any title insurance company can give you a quote for owners' and for lenders' basic title insurance. They will need to know the purchase price and the amount of the mortgage loan. Remember, though, this will not include extra endorsements requested by your particular lender.

The local office where deeds and mortgages are recorded can tell you how to calculate recording fees and transfer taxes. These are usually a percentage of the dollar amount of the transaction.

What happens after closing?

After closing, you are officially an investor, which means you are responsible for taking care of your investment. The next section will answer questions about how to do so.

Chapter 26

TENANT SELECTION—MAKE WISE CHOICES TO PRESERVE VALUE

- I thought I was not allowed to discriminate against tenants. Is that true?
- What things do I want to think about in choosing among potential tenants?
- Can I screen tenants for bad credit risks, criminal backgrounds, and other such things?
- If I discover I made a mistake in renting to someone, do I have to let him or her renew his or her lease?

Making the right rental decisions can be the key to investment success or failure. One poor tenant choice can condemn you to similar tenants for the rest of the time you own your property. As an example, suppose you buy a small strip center and have plans for an upscale, boutique-type tenant mix. But, you have a few vacancies that you need to fill with someone willing to pay the rent on time. As a result, you put a tattoo parlor at one end. At the other end, you sign up a payday advance company. There is nothing wrong with these businesses, but they will definitely deter an expensive women's boutique from taking space. That is what is normally meant by *tenant selection*.

I thought I was not allowed to discriminate against tenants. Is that true?

You are not allowed to make decisions based on someone's status as one of what is called the *suspect classifications*. They are such things as race, gender, family status, and disability. Those issuess are covered in more detail in Appendix B. You can discriminate on the basis that someone is a poor business risk or not right for your ideal tenant mix as long as your reason is not an excuse for illegal discrimination.

What things do I want to think about in choosing among potential tenants?

The following is a checklist of items to consider. Not all of them will apply to all situations. They will, however, help your mind start working in the right direction.

- Is this tenant's business compatible with my other tenants' customers and clients? (Would the clientele of an upscale women's clothing store be compatible with that of the tattoo parlor?)

- Does this business compete with a tenant I already have or one that I hope to obtain in the near future? (Do you want to rent space to Kathy's Koffee Klatch if you think you might have a chance to get Starbucks instead?)

- What are the parking needs for this tenant? (Will this tenant's customers fill the parking lot and cause problems for my other tenants?)

- Will this tenant's activities generate large amounts of noise, trash, electricity consumption, or possible negative advertising (e.g., a recording studio or an abortion clinic)?

- Will this tenant create an image I do not want? (What kind of reputation will a high concentration of alcoholic beverage vendors at one location give your property?)

- Is this tenant likely to outgrow my space fairly quickly and leave? (Depending on your situation, you might want to wait for a more long-term tenant.)

- Is this tenant likely to grow to the point that it wants to buy my building in the future? (Again, depending on your future plans, this may be a good thing.)
- Is this tenant a good credit risk?

- Is this tenant likely to cause excessive wear and tear to the property (e.g., a day care center)?

- Is this tenant likely to increase my fire insurance premiums (e.g., a restaurant)?

• Is this tenant likely to attract vermin (e.g., a restaurant or seed/feed store)?

Can I screen tenants for bad credit risks, criminal backgrounds, and other such things?

You can refuse to rent to someone because of bad credit or a criminal background so long as you have firm rules and do not apply them on a case-by-case basis. There are many commercial services that provide these kinds of background checks for you or that make them available online. Check with other landlords or property management firms in your town for guidance regarding which resources they find most useful.

If I discover I made a mistake in renting to someone, do I have to let him or her renew his or her lease?

Do not be afraid to refuse to renew a problem tenant. You have to weigh all the headaches of having that tenant against the financial pain of having empty space for a few months until you find a new one.

Chapter 27

RENTAL RATES AND SECURITY DEPOSITS— WHAT IS FAIR?

- How much rent should I charge for residential properties?
- How much rent should I charge for business properties?
- If I meet price resistance, should I lower my price?
- How much security deposit should I collect?
- How do I handle requests for security deposit waivers?
- When should I refund the security deposit?
- How often should I raise rents?

Choosing the right asking price can be tricky and stressful. Ask too little, and you leave money on the table. Ask too much, and you chill the marketplace, scaring away potential buyers or tenants. Navigate successfully through these shoals with the advice below.

How much rent should I charge for residential properties?

Your ideal rent will be determined by your marketplace and your personal sales skills. Start by researching the marketplace; find out what other people with similar properties charge.

The key is knowing your competition. Find out what properties are available for rent in your same general area, what features they have, and what the monthly rates are. Make calls to other rental property owners, introduce yourself as another landlord, explain you are trying to keep up with the marketplace, and ask your questions. People are generally very cooperative and helpful. The better you know your competition, the more likely you are to become allies, working together on common problems. An added bonus is that when you are ready to sell, you will probably approach the other local landlords first to offer your property for sale, and potentially save money on real estate commissions.

How much rent should I charge for business properties?

In most markets, *business properties* are separated by type, then by quality. Rents are based on a certain amount per square foot, depending on the general type and quality of property.

Some different types of small investor business properties are:

- professional office
- medical office
- convenience store
- fast food out-parcel

- neighborhood office
- store-front office
- converted house/boutique
- small retail
- strip center

- restaurant
- self-storage
- parking lots
- boat slips
- flea market/antique mall

Quality is dependent on the market. Many years ago, in Houston, Texas, top law firm offices had leather wall coverings, marble floors throughout, exotic wood trim, hand-etched glass in interior walls, ballroom staircases between floors, and at least one conference room with a twenty-foot ceiling. That was considered "Class A" office space. In Alabama, on the other hand, that kind of office would have been considered a house of ill repute, if you could even find anything like it in the area. Get a feel for the different grades of property in your markeplace, and then separate them into A, B, and C properties.

Next, you will need to make some phone calls to properties that are the same general grade as your own and in your submarket. A *submarket* is a self-contained, well-defined area. You would not call landlords in Manhattan if your property was in Queens, for example. Find out how many square feet are in the space available for rent, the amount of the monthly rent, and if that rent is for a one-, three-, or five-year lease. Generally speaking, leases for shorter terms charge higher rents. Smaller spaces rent for a higher per-square foot rate than larger space. The *breaking points* for rents, which are the divisions of square feet that usually help to determine the amount of rent, are generally:

- 50–300 square feet
- 300–1,000 square feet
- 1,000–5,000 square feet
- 5,000–20,000 square feet

- 20,000–100,000 square feet
- 100,000+ square feet

Something that further complicates rents on business properties is the *common area maintenance* (CAM). When doing your research, find out if your competitors' rents include charges for exterior lighting, parking lot cleaning, janitorial service, garbage pickup, and other things. Two buildings, side by side, might have completely different rents for their offices. The difference could be in whether tenants also pay extra for the common area maintenance, or if that is included in their basic monthly rent.

When you are finished, you will have a list of properties similar to your own, the number of square feet in them, and the monthly rent. By convention, most of the United States quotes rent as a dollar amount per square foot per *year*. There are some exceptions that quote rent as a dollar amount per square foot per *month*. You will just have to ask someone how they do things in your community. Any commercial property manager can tell you that.

If you found three offices for rent, one with 1,000 square feet at $1,900 per month, one with 800 square feet at $1,525 per month, and one with 1,200 square feet at $2,300 per month, then the average rent is $23 per foot. Here are the calculations:

$1,900 per month x 12 months = $22,800 per year
$22,800 per year ÷ 1,000 square feet = $22.80 per square foot rent
$1,525 per month x 12 months = $18,300 per year
$18,300 ÷ 800 square feet = $22.87 per square foot rent
$2,300 per month x 12 months = $27,600 per year
$27,600 ÷ 1,200 square feet = $23 per square foot rent

You should charge $23 per square foot per year for your rent, and then divide that number by 12 to arrive at the monthly rent.

If I meet price resistance, should I lower my price?

If you have done your homework properly, the rent you are quoting should be consistent with the marketplace. If you meet price resistance, say something like this: "I am a new investor, and perhaps I did not do a very good job researching what other landlords of similar properties charge. Do you mind sharing with me some information regarding who is charging the amount you say is fair for my property?" This either calls their bluff, or gives you additional information with which to do a reality check on your rates.

Sometimes, your asking rent is fair but you are afraid of losing a prospective tenant. Lowering your rate is not the answer. Instead, offer the first month free, the first month at half price, or some other incentive that works out the same for the tenant.

Example: You are asking $1,100 per month for your house. The prospect says he or she cannot afford to go over $1,000 per month. The annual savings to that person is $1,200 at his or her price. If that is agreeable to you, give him or her the first month free ($1,100) instead. The dollars work out pretty much the same, but:

- "First month free" will usually cinch a deal because, for the tenant, it is like finding that much money on the sidewalk. Now the tenant can go out and spend $1,100 on things he or she wants.

- If you reduce your rent to $1,000, and next year the market rate for your house is $1,200, you will probably not be able to bump your tenant up by $200. Psychologically, it is too much of an increase. You will either lose the tenant, or raise the rent only $100 a month. This can continue for many years, with you undercharging $1,200 per year in rents.

How much security deposit should I collect?

Many state laws limit you to one month's rent as a security deposit for residential properties. Even if you are legally allowed to charge more, one month seems to be the norm.

States that do not have the security deposit limit are usually the ones that have not passed any uniform landlord/tenant legislation. As a result, they are usually also the ones with outdated eviction procedures that can take up to six months, with the tenant paying no rent in the meantime. If you are in a state without security deposit caps and you have a tenant prospect with a poor credit history, obtain at least two months' rent as a deposit.

Landlords for business properties usually charge two months' rent as a security deposit.

> **Tip:** Never waive the security deposit. You never know what is going to happen. After going through the bank failures in Texas in the 1980s, I can tell you from experience that the best tenants in the world *might* default. The ones who seem least likely to break their lease are the ones most financially able to pay the deposit, anyway. They are just bargaining with you, trying to obtain a concession.

Even without business failure, large corporations are the worst ones about paying their bills on time because of high turnover in their accounts payable departments. They are also the ones who will simply ignore your bills for late charges month after month and then, at the end of their lease term, practically dare you to sue them over the money. You both know you cannot afford to tackle them in court. You lose the money, unless you have a security deposit.

How do I handle requests for security deposit waivers?

One of the ways I deal with requests to waive security deposits is to write a new clause into the lease. It says that if the rent is ever received by me on the sixth day of the month or later, the tenant will have to pay the security deposit. I make it the tenant's problem to get that money to me on time. If he or she has to overnight it each month, just so it is not delayed in the mail, that is the tenant's headache, not mine.

Some tenants truly cannot afford the entire security deposit, up front. They will not be able to rent your property if you insist on it. In those circumstances, I charge the full security deposit, but collect only a portion in advance. The remainder is billed to the tenant over the next two or three months. If the tenant prospect cannot afford that, he or she cannot afford your property. That person is living too much on the outer edge of his or her finances. One blip in his or her life, and you will not receive his or her rent check on the first of the month.

When should I refund the security deposit?

You should refund the security deposit within a reasonable time after the end of the lease term. Give yourself time to inspect the premises and make sure there is no damage caused by the tenant. Many states have laws setting a time limit for residential security deposits, usually within forty-five days of lease end.

Never, never, never refund the security deposit before the lease expires. A tenant who has paid his or her rent on time every month for three years might still default if his or her financial situation changes. Plus, you do not know what damage he or she might cause to the property.

How often should I raise rents?

You should raise rents at least once a year. If you have multi-year leases, include an automatic rent increase on the anniversary date each year. How much of a rent increase will depend on the annual increases in your marketplace. Most small investors have at least a 3% annual increase.

Many leases include clauses raising the rents in a proportionate amount if the real estate tax or insurance goes up on the property. You have no control over those expenses, which could rise dramatically. A mere 3% annual increase will not protect you if insurance premiums double or triple because of some catastrophe in the area.

Chapter 28

PROPERTY MANAGEMENT COMPANIES— TAKING CARE OF BUSINESS

■ Should I hire a property management company?

■ What does a property management company do?

■ How do I choose a good property management company?

■ When hiring a property management firm, what contract clauses should be given special consideration?

At some point in your investing career, you will outgrow your own management efforts and need to hire full-time employees or a management company. A management company is the logical first step because it can act without your regular supervision, it brings a wealth of experience, training, forms, and procedures to the table, and because it will be cheaper than an employee with office space and equipment.

Should I hire a property management company?

Most beginning investors manage their rental properties themselves until the time demands become a burden. Everyone will have a different breaking point, where paying someone else 5%–10% of gross revenues is worth it because you can do other things with your time. For some people, that breaking point occurs with the very first investment. Your time is better spent finding new deals than screening potential tenants and unclogging toilets, especially if your goal is to quickly build a sizeable portfolio.

What does a property management company do?

Property managers usually offer a menu of services. Your fee depends on how many you choose. They can do everything from finding tenants to collecting rents to handling complaints and routine maintenance/repair issues to evictions. Good property management firms provide all legal forms and notices required to manage the property and make sure that all federal, state, and local laws are followed. They can shop for the best insurance and repairs, help you fight unfair increases in property taxes, and make recommendations regarding keeping your rents at market rates. The best ones will advise you regarding additional income opportunities such as laundromats, reselling Internet access, and furniture rental. They will also tell you about additional investment opportunities, and when it is the right time to sell your investments and trade up to something better.

How do I choose a good property management company?

When interviewing property management firms, ask about the firms' years of experience, and the experience of the current operations personnel. It does you no good to hire a management company with twenty years of experience if all line employees have little experience and no in-house training. Inquire about how many units they manage and for how many different owners. A company that manages two hundred units might have one apartment complex owned by the firm itself. Ask for proof of liability insurance and for references, and actually check the references.

Inquire into the services they offer and about success stories in which they saved money for their clients or prevented problems. Stress that you do not want any names, just examples. Anyone who is good at what he or she does will have thought about these things and reflected on the good job he or she does for his or her clients. If the firm cannot share any success stories with you, you should rethink doing business with them.

Ask for a few horror stories regarding other management firms, or people who self-manage. Again, be sure to mention that you do not want any names. A management firm that is in touch with its community should know those things. You want someone who can justify the good he or she can do for you.

> **Tip:** I usually ask each company what makes it better than its competition. Good firms have good, thoughtful responses to this question. Those are the ones you want to choose, so long as you can confirm that their responses are accurate.

The national trade association for property managers is the Institute of Real Estate Management (IREM). Its website at **www.irem.org** includes a tab at the top of the page for owners/investors and information relevant to them.

When hiring a property management firm, what contract clauses should be given special consideration?

Most people hiring a property management firm pay attention to the percentage of rent the company charges for its services. You should also be sure to ask the following questions.

- What are all the additional charges that might appear on my monthly bill? (Do you charge separately for phone calls, copies, mileage, generating reports, conducting inspections, collections activities, repairs performed by your own personnel, etc.?)

- What other people do you typically hire to perform services or supply goods that will be rebilled to me? How are those people or companies related to you, if at all?

- What additional fees might you charge tenants besides the monthly rent? Do you keep those fees, or are they additional income?

- What fees do you charge prospective tenants, such as for credit checks? Who keeps that money?

- Is there a minimum term to our contract, or can I cancel at any time, for any reason? If I do cancel at any time, do I have to pay a termination fee? If so, how is it calculated? (This is usually fair because the property manager does not want to train you in what he or she does, and then have you cancel the contract when you think you have obtained copies of all the company's forms and learned everything it can teach you.)

- What are the circumstances under which I can cancel "for cause" because you are not doing your job properly, and have no further obligations under the contract?

Chapter 29

INSURANCE AND RISK MANAGEMENT

- When should I begin shopping for insurance?
- What kinds of insurance do I need?
- If I sell investment property and hold the financing, what do I need to know about insurance?
- Do I need title insurance?
- What is private mortgage insurance?
- What other insurance might be useful?

Insurance is one tool in your kit of *risk management* strategies. It is always comforting to have property insurance in case you suffer a fire loss, but it is even better if you never have a fire in the first place. Learning to avoid or minimize risks, and then having adequate insurance for the surprises, is the focus of this chapter.

When should I begin shopping for insurance?

The best time to shop for insurance is before you sign a contract to buy a piece of property. A good insurance agent can give you valuable advice regarding the best types of properties that will minimize your insurance expenses. An insurance company prefers properties that are fairly "bullet proof." It offers the best rates for those types of property. Use your insurance agent as an advisor.

The annual insurance premiums on a property can make or break a deal. Learn about the premiums before you become obligated under a purchase contract.

For any property you have under consideration, require the seller to provide you with a *C.L.U.E. report*, which is the insurance claims report for the property for the past five years. If there has been water damage, you might have black mold issues. A fire could indicate structural concerns. You may also discover that the current owner has renewed the insurance for years, but a new owner might not be able to obtain insurance on that property for various reasons. An insurance agent can review the report and advise you.

What kinds of insurance do I need?

The best kind of general property insurance policy is called an *all-risks policy* or a *comprehensive policy*. It covers every disaster and damage except those specifically excluded by the policy. Cheaper policies might have a long list of things that are covered, but if anything else happens, you have no insurance coverage.

Be sure to obtain policy limits high enough to replace your property if it is totally destroyed. You can increase those limits each year as your property increases in value, or you can obtain coverage that automatically increases according to inflation. The automatic increases are nice because you do not have to think about them, but they will not give you enough protection if your property is increasing in value more rapidly than general inflation.

Flood insurance is available from the federal government. Lenders require it for any property that has a 1% likelihood of flooding in any given year. This is popularly known as "being in the 100-year flood plain." Even if not required, property owners might want to consider obtaining flood insurance anyway. The premium is usually around $500 per year for the average home or other small property. According to the Federal Emergency Management Agency (FEMA), 25% of flood claims are for properties in low- to moderate-risk areas. You can obtain more information by visiting the website of the National Flood Insurance Program at **www.floodsmart.gov**.

Specialized landlord insurance protects your property and provides additional coverage for loss of income during un-rentable periods or sometimes during disputes with tenants. In the alternative, you might need a *general business liability policy* (GBL). Make sure you are covered against claims for personal injuries, defamation, wrongful eviction, conversion (claims that you took a tenant's personal property), mental distress, and violation of fair housing laws. You might also want to think about riders for employee dishonesty and for off-premises use of vehicles by an employee.

If you have employees, such as your own property manager or maintenance person, your state may require *workers' compensation insurance*. Having workers' compensation insurance results in employee work-related medical bills and personal injury claims being paid, even if your employee was at fault for his or her own injuries. This might not seem fair, but the tradeoff is that you are protected against lawsuits, even if the injury was clearly *your* fault. The employee is not allowed to sue you for his or her injuries or losses. He or she is limited to the workers' compensation coverage, or can argue with and sue the workers' compensation company.

If I sell investment property and hold the financing, what do I need to know about insurance?

If you sell property and hold the financing, make sure you are named as an additional insured on the purchaser's policy. There are two types of lender coverages. One is called the *standard mortgage clause*, or sometimes the *union clause*. It allows the mortgage lender to recover even if the borrower/property owner is guilty of some wrongdoing that would void the policy. The other type, called the *open mortgage clause*, results in no lender coverage if the borrower was guilty of arson, for example. Neither one will provide coverage if the borrower fails to pay the premium, however. You will need to monitor that situation. The insurance company should give you notice of cancellation if that is in danger of happening, but you must make sure the company has a current address for you.

Do I need title insurance?

You should always obtain *title insurance* when you buy property and again if you sell property and hold the financing. The first kind is an *owners' policy*, and the second kind is called a *lenders' policy*. They protect you against claims that another person has a better right than you to the property. Examples of problems covered include the following.

- The prior owner had an IRS lien filed against the property before the sale. The IRS was not paid out of sale proceeds, so the lien is still on the property.

- Someone performed work on the property, such as repairs, and was not paid by the prior owner. Those workers can usually file a lien against the property up to six months after the work was performed, even if the real estate has changed hands. This is called a *mechanics' and materialmen's lien.*

- Your purchase at a property tax sale was invalid because the authorities did not give proper notice to the prior owner.

- An IRS lien continues on a foreclosed property, even though the lien was filed after the mortgage (and should have been wiped out by the foreclosure) because the lender did not give the proper pre-foreclosure notice to the IRS.

- A prior owner sold the property, but did not include his or her spouse's signature on the deed. As a result, the spouse still has claims to the property, even though the property was never in his or her name.

The title insurance company will pay all expenses to defend your claim. If that is not successful, it will pay off the other claimant for the value of his or her claim.

What is private mortgage insurance?

Private mortgage insurance, also called PMI, protects the lender in case there is a foreclosure and the property does not sell for enough money to pay off the debt. When buying a home with less than an 20% down payment, most lenders will require you to purchase, and pay the premiums on, private mortgage insurance. This is rarely a requirement for investor loans. If you sell property and hold the financing, you will probably not be able to obtain PMI insurance to protect yourself. The largest company in that industry, by far, is Mortgage Guaranty Insurance Corporation (MGIC). It reports that it does not write policies for private lenders—seller financing. You can obtain more information by visiting its website at **www.mgic.com**.

What other insurance might be useful?

If you self-manage your property full-time, you might want to look into disability insurance. Hiring someone else to take care of your chores can become very expensive. Make sure your policy covers *own occ*, meaning you collect if you are disabled from performing your own occupation. The much less useful *all occ* policy pays only if you are completely disabled and cannot perform any occupation at all.

Chapter 30

WORKING WITHOUT AN AGENT—ADVICE FOR SELLERS

- How much should I ask for my property?
- What information do I need for a buyer?
- How can I expose my property to the marketplace?
- How can I avoid wasting time with sightseers?
- Should I call people back who did not seem interested when I first spoke with them?
- What do I do if someone makes a verbal offer that seems acceptable?
- What is the best way to counteroffer if the original purchase offer is not acceptable?
- Who should hold the earnest money?
- Who makes sure everything happens on time through the closing?

You may find yourself wanting to sell your real estate without listing it with a broker, especially if your investment strategy calls for flipping properties. A little preparation ahead of time, good exposure, and organized follow-up procedures will work wonders for you.

How much should I ask for my property?

Refer to Chapter 18 for a more detailed answer to this question. The simple answer is: *Ask for what the property is worth.* Too many people place a value according to what they *need* to get in order to make a profit, buy things they want to buy, or pay off their credit cards. None of these things are relevant to a property's value. Others play games, asking an unrealistic price but being prepared to reduce it dramatically if an offer comes in. The best strategy is to ask a fair price, be willing to reduce it a very small amount if necessary, and then stick to your guns.

What information do I need for a buyer?

You should assemble all your information first, before you take the first step in marketing your property. You should be ready if the first person you speak with asks for an information package.

The contents of the package will vary depending on the type of property. At a minimum, you want the street address, legal description, some color photos, asking price, willingness to pay a commission (if you decide to do that), approximate size of the lot, general description of any improvements you have made to the property, and approximate square footage of the improvements.

An information package for a home should generally include all relevant school districts, average utility costs for twelve months (if known), and distance to shopping, fast-food restaurants, the fire station, and other relevant points. Information about income-producing property would include zoning for the property, availability of high-speed

Internet, names of any commercial tenants—but not names of individuals renting dwellings—and a twelve-month operating statement or a projected twelve-month pro forma if the property is unoccupied.

> **Tip:** Use an accountant to help you prepare this information. Many owners have failed to receive full value for their property simply because financial data was presented in the wrong manner. For example, replacing the roof is something for which you write a check. It is not, however, an operating expense, and therefore should not be included on your operating statement. Putting it there will cause a potential buyer to think your property is much less profitable than it really is, which can dramatically reduce his or her offering price.

Demographic information is often very important when marketing a commercial property. This is the profile of the area within a one-, three-, and five-mile radius. It includes average income, household sizes, ages of people in the area, and an incredible variety of other information. You can order demographic reports from Claritas, which is the largest paid provider of that information. More information is available from **www.claritas.com**.

Traffic counts are also useful. Call your local Department of Transportation and ask how you can obtain those numbers. They show how many vehicles pass certain points within a twenty-four hour period. This is extremely important to many potential buyers.

If you are selling raw land, mention what utilities are on the property, which ones come to the property, and which ones are nearby. Zoning information is important, as well as whether the property is within any city limits or police jurisdictions. Include traffic counts, if known. Any surveys or topographical maps you have available for inspection should be mentioned.

How can I expose my property to the marketplace?

First, find out the names and addresses of the property owners neighboring your own. Adjoining property owners are the easiest potential buyers to find, and the fastest closes at the best prices. Do not rely on these people to contact you after you put up a "For Sale" sign. Many will wait several months before calling you, afraid to look too eager. If you call them, however, they will know you are aggressive and motivated, and they will believe that failure to make an offer quickly could result in someone else buying the property.

Expanding outward beyond your immediate neighbors, other area homeowners usually know friends and relatives who want to live in the neighborhood. Landlords in the same general area are usually eager to acquire additional properties. Tenants often want to stay in the same part of town, and may be ready to move up to home ownership. These people should all be your next contacts, generally by way of a flyer put in a noticeable place, such as in the screen door.

> **Note:** If you believe that a contact is out of town, you should still distribute a flyer to his or her residence, but make sure it is in a spot that is inconspicuous from the street. There is no faster way to generate animosity than by taping a flyer on the front door of someone's house who is on vacation. After a few days, it is a neon sign to burglars.

If these efforts do not result in significant interest in two weeks or so, move on to the next step. Establish a marketing budget. Once you determine how much money you can spend, decide the best places to spend it. This may be a little bit of a chicken-and-egg situation, because you first need to have a general idea about how much different strategies and advertising media cost. The smaller your budget, the more creative you will need to be and the more of your personal time you will have to spend in getting the word out.

> **Tip:** It is a truism in real estate brokerage that classified ads and open houses are a waste of time. They are done to satisfy the property owner, who is able to see some evidence of agent activity. They rarely result in buyers for that property.

Targeted outreach can be very successful. This is like what you did when you went to the neighbors. Expand that concept. Who is likely to want to buy your property? If it is a good retail location, a successful business in some other part of town or a nearby community might want to expand to your location.

Almost all cities and towns have real estate brokers who will charge you a flat fee to place your property on the local MLS service. Compare prices and terms—does your fee buy you six months on MLS, or an indefinite time period until the property sells? Prominently disclose that you will pay a 3%—or whatever you want—commission to any agent who brings a buyer to the closing table. You need to give some incentive, otherwise there is no practical reason why an agent would do you a favor and tell his or her buyers about your listing. This is not a public service agents provide—it is a career. The downside is that any potential buyers working without an agent will know you are willing to reduce your price by that amount if you do not have to pay a commission.

Try to obtain placement on all websites your budget will afford you. According to the National Association of REALTORS®, 87% of home buyers find their properties on the Internet. There are many different websites devoted to commercial listings such as apartments, offices, and retail space. LoopNet, at **www.loopnet.com**, is one of the largest.

How can I avoid wasting time with sightseers?

The sightseers, or tourists, are not real prospects. They enjoy looking at properties and dreaming about buying something, but they are never going to actually make a decision. Other times, they cannot possibly afford your property and their financial planning hinges on some sort of a financial miracle happening.

In order to work as efficiently as possible, you need to learn how to recognize these people as soon as possible. Rather than passively answering their questions, immediately take control of the conversation and begin asking some of your own. Most callers want to know the price—it is usually their first question. Some people tell you to wait until later in the conversation to divulge that information. The thinking is that you should sell the caller on all the benefits of your property before disclosing the price. In that way, you meet much less resistance.

I do not think you are going to sell anything over the phone. That first phone call is to weed out the obvious tourists and obtain contact information for the possibly qualified buyers. When someone asks the price, I first ask his or her name and phone number, in case we are disconnected. Write it down, plus the number on the caller ID if it is different. Then I say, "I am selling the property for $228,000, which is the appraised value. Is that figure within the amount you have budgeted for a property of this type?" In this manner, you answer a question, ask your own question, and maintain control of the conversation afterward. You want to be the one asking questions, not the other way around. Read more about this in Chapter 19.

Should I call people back who did not seem interested when I first spoke with them?

By all means, follow up with potential buyers if they leave the door open even a crack. Even if they were very negative with you at first, their plans or expectations might have changed in the meantime.

The person who thought he or she could buy a four-bedroom, three-bathroom house in a good school zone for $49,000 might have received a good dose of reality since your last conversation.

What do I do if someone makes a verbal offer that seems acceptable?

Ideally, you would like all offers to be in writing so there is no misunderstanding. On the other hand, I am hesitant to ask prospects to put their offers in writing. That little bit of extra work and time could cost the deal if they find something they like better, or if their influences talk them out of buying your property. When faced with a verbal offer, ask the potential buyer if you could reduce that to writing and get it to him or her as soon as possible for signature. That way, you control the timing and a lot of the additional terms in the offer.

An offer should also be in writing so that, if it is acceptable, you can then sign it and thereby create a binding contract. Verbal contracts are not enforceable if they have to do with buying or selling real estate.

Review Chapter 16, which addresses buyers who work without an agent. All the contract clauses in that chapter are perfectly reasonable clauses for both sides. As a seller, you want to limit the due diligence to something as short as possible, and you want to obtain the largest earnest money deposit you think you can negotiate. You should also reserve the right to continue marketing the property, and to accept back-up contracts in case the current one falls through.

What is the best way to counteroffer if the original purchase offer is not acceptable?

In order to avoid confusion, draw a red line through the middle of any language you find objectionable. Do not completely obliterate it, because you might need to reconstruct the course of negotiations later, in case there is a dispute. Put the date and your initials next to everything you line out.

Above the signature lines, write in red, *See Attached Addendum*. Mark a clean sheet of paper as "Addendum," and write in your replacement language, with initials and the date next to each section. Keep doing things in this same manner until you have reached an agreement on all points. You can use the same addendum sheet for all replacement language—just make sure you line out and date the rejected items and date the replacements. When the last person makes a change that is agreed upon, the other one must initial and date the change, which creates a fully executed contract. Because of technicalities of contract law, if you do not do this, you will not have an enforceable agreement.

Who should hold the earnest money?

A disinterested third party should hold the earnest money. That could be an escrow company, the attorney who will handle the closing, or someone else with a separate bank account for escrow funds.

Who makes sure everything happens on time through the closing?

Making sure everything occurs exactly as the contract specifies takes a lot of work. Agree with the buyer on a closing company. It is illegal under federal law—the *Real Estate Settlement and Procedures Act* (RESPA)—for the seller to *require* in the contract that the parties use a specific closing company. Meet with someone from that firm as soon as possible and ask him or her to give you a list of what needs to be done, and in what order. I am never bashful about asking the buyer if he or she will give me his or her lender's closing requirements checklist. Many of the items on the list can easily be provided by the seller, which saves time for everyone.

Chapter 31

TAXES— ADDITIONAL BENEFITS TO INVESTING IN REAL ESTATE

- How can owning real estate reduce my income taxes?
- What is depreciation?
- What are some other deductions I can take?
- Is there a downside to depreciation deductions?
- Are there any limits on my deductions?
- What are the most common tax credits?
- Can I take advantage of long-term capital gains tax rates?
- What is a 1031 (tax free) exchange?
- Can a Subchapter S corporation save taxes for me?
- What is all the GO Zone hype I'm reading about?

Having a good general knowledge of tax law is what separates the amateur investor from the real winner. The U.S. government is firmly in favor of widespread investment in real estate. As a result, it offers an incredible array of tax benefits to encourage people to buy homes and invest in real estate. The following answer questions about some of the most common tax benefits.

How can owning real estate reduce my income taxes?

There are five ways that owning real estate can reduce your income taxes.

1. Depreciation deductions each year allow you to write off part of the cost of your investment, resulting in lower taxable income and lower taxes. If you have a $1,000 tax deduction, it means that $1,000 of your income will be tax-free. This is called *sheltering*. In addition, virtually all expenses associated with owning and operating investment properties, including mortgage interest, are deductible.

2. Some real estate investments give you tax credits. Tax credits are used to reduce your tax liability. Dollar for dollar, these are more valuable than deductions. If you are in the 28% tax bracket, then a $1,000 tax credit means that $3,571.43 of your income will be tax-free. (Twenty-eight percent of $3,571.43 is $1,000. You would have to pay $1,000 in taxes on $3,571.43, but the tax credit wipes out your tax liability.)

3. Currently, you can sell your primary residence every two years and make up to $250,000 in profit ($500,000 for married couples) and pay absolutely no income taxes, ever.

4. With *capital gains* tax rates, you can sell real estate after owning it for one year and pay taxes at a greatly reduced rate. Right now, the highest tax rate for individuals' *ordinary income* (wages, salary, rents from property, interest, dividends, etc.) is 35%. The highest capital gains tax rate is only 15%.

5. Real estate offers some wonderful opportunities for estate planning and reduction of taxes. The details are beyond the scope of this book, but you can put business or investment real estate in the name of a family limited liability partnership and make annual gifts of shares of that company to family members and other persons you want to benefit from your estate. If the gifts are under the size limits, there is no gift tax owed by you and no income tax owed by the recipient. You retain control of everything. No one can ever vote you out of control. But due to the magic of appraisal techniques and IRS incentives, a 90% ownership share of $1 million of real estate ($900,000, ordinarily) might have an estate tax value of only $540,000. This can dramatically reduce estate taxes, with a little planning. For details, go to the IRS webpage at **www.irs.gov**.

What is depreciation?

Technically, *depreciation* is an accounting term. The IRS equivalent, which gives you tax deductions, is called *cost recovery*. You will need to know both phrases if you are doing Internet research. In common speech, though, everyone just refers to both of them as *depreciation*.

Depreciation is an agreed-upon fiction that your real estate improvements—not the land itself, but everything else—are becoming less valuable every year at a steady rate. The IRS is of the opinion that residential rental properties will last for 27.5 years after you buy or build them and then be worthless. The IRS also allows you to pretend that commercial properties will last for 39 years, and convenience stores will have no value after 15 years. As a result, you are allowed to write off, as a deduction, the pro rata amount that the property loses in value each year.

You can increase your deductions if you take advantage of something called *cost allocation depreciation*. With this, some components of your property improvements can be split out and depreciated more quickly than the whole. Carpets, exterior lighting, fencing, security systems, and other items can be depreciated over five, seven, or fifteen years, for example. Talk to an accountant or do a good bit of research before taking this route, however. Guessing incorrectly can result in audits, fines, and penalties.

What are some other deductions I can take?

Virtually everything associated with operating, insuring, protecting, repairing, or managing investment real estate can be deducted as an expense. Some items that add to the property or extend its life, such as a new roof or a building addition, cannot be deducted. Instead, you have to depreciate them a little bit, each year. This is an area that might require some accounting assistance. For a general overview, read IRS Publication 527, "Residential Rental Property," and IRS Publication 946, "How to Depreciate Property," for more details. They are available at **www.irs.gov** for download, or by calling 800-829-1040 to request that a copy be mailed to you.

Is there a downside to depreciation deductions?

There is not really a downside, but just a consequence that many people do not really think about. It makes logical sense, once someone explains it, but it might not occur to you ahead of time.

Example: Suppose you pay $65,000 for a rental house. You own it for exactly one year, and you sell it for $65,000. There is no gain, so you have no taxable income on the transaction.

But, what if you owned the rental house for just over a year and wrote off $2,000 in depreciation deductions? You get the benefit of $2,000 worth of tax benefits in the current year. The IRS will not let you sell the property for $65,000 and pay no income taxes. It says, "You received $2,000 worth of tax benefits last year, so we are going to take back some of those benefits this year."

For purposes of calculating gain on the sale, you have to subtract that $2,000 from your $65,000 purchase price and treat the property as if you bought it for only $63,000, which gives you a gain of $2,000.

This is called your *basis*. Every year that you take depreciation deductions—but not any other normal expenses—you have to reduce your basis in the same amount as the depreciation deductions.

Based on the example, you might think that depreciation does not help you at all. However, it really does. You receive tax deductions against each year's taxable income. You save money at your highest tax rate for that year. While you pay taxes in a later year when you sell the property, (1) inflation makes your dollars worth less in the future; (2) if you qualify for long-term capital gains tax rates, then the highest tax rate is 15% instead of the highest individual tax rate of 35%, which means your deductions save you money at 35%, and paying taxes later costs you only 15%; and, (3) if you use something called a *1031 exchange*, then you do not have to pay any taxes at all, even when you sell the property.

Are there any limits on my deductions?

There are two limits on your deductions. One is caused by calculations performed under the *alternative minimum tax rules*, or *Alt-Min* for short. The other limit has to do with something called the *passive activity rules*. Neither one of these rules affects how much your property deductions can reduce your property income. They both affect how much *other* income you can shelter with your real estate deductions.

Under Alt-Min, certain tax deductions, called *tax preference items*, are given limited effect. Depreciation is a tax preference item. The alternative minimum tax law was passed in 1969 in order to prevent a few wealthy individuals from escaping income taxes completely by virtue of their many deductions. The rules never changed to account for inflation, though. The annual income of a wealthy individual in 1969 is equivalent to a normal two-income earning family in today's world, which means that average Americans are being caught in the Alt-Min trap. The *New York Times* estimates that, by 2010, nearly thirty million Americans will have to pay additional taxes because of the alternative minimum tax.

The Alt-Min calculations are complex. Fortunately, the IRS provides an electronic worksheet, called the *Alternative Minimum Tax Assistant*, online at **www.irs.gov**. It lets you adjust your numbers to see what happens. Do not worry—the IRS cannot tell who is online using the forms. No information will be collected and matched against your actual tax returns later. You can also download Topic 556, "Alternative Minimum Tax," from the IRS website for a better understanding of the rules.

The IRS makes a distinction between certain types of income and expenses, especially those it considers a result of so-called *passive activities*. Passive activity expenses are deductible only from passive activity income. If expenses exceed income, then the losses cannot be used to offset other income, such as payroll income. Instead, the passive activity losses have to be carried forward and used in future tax years. Rental activities are considered passive activities. As an example, if you have $35,000 of expenses associated with rental properties—because of depreciation deductions—and only $12,000 of income, then you will not pay any taxes on the $12,000. But, you cannot use the remaining $23,000 to reduce the taxable income from your day job.

The good news is that there are three exceptions to passive activities.

1. Taxpayers may deduct up to $12,500 in passive losses (up to $25,000 for married couples) if they or their spouse actively participated in the activity.

2. If the rental is a dwelling the taxpayer uses for more than fourteen days per year, or 10% of the days the dwelling is available for rental (whichever is greater), then it does not count as a passive activity. This would be your beach house, for example.

3. The taxpayer is a real estate professional, which, for these purposes, means someone who performed more than 750 hours of services that year in real property trades or businesses in which he or she materially participated, *and* more than half the personal services the taxpayer performed in all trades or businesses were performed in real property trades or businesses.

For more information on this, see IRS Publication 925, "Passive Activity and the At-Risk Rules," and Tax Topic 425, "Passive Activities—Losses and Credits," at the IRS website, **www.irs.gov**.

What are the most common tax credits?

A tax credit reduces your bottom line tax liability. One dollar in tax credits saves you one dollar in taxes, which is different from a deduction in which a one-dollar deduction might save you fifteen to thirty-five cents in taxes.

The three most common tax credits available to investors in real estate are:

1. *rehabilitation tax credit* (see Chapter 3 on fixer-uppers for more details);

2. *energy efficiency tax credit* (for installing energy efficient systems and appliances); and,

3. *low-income housing tax credits*, which is a time-consuming but extremely profitable strategy. Although the credits are for your federal income taxes, you must call your *state* low-income housing agency for more details. The IRS gives the credits to the states, and then the states award them to applicants. See, also, HUD information available at **www.huduser.org/datasets/lihtc.html**.

Can I take advantage of long-term capital gains tax rates?

Yes, anyone can take advantage of the reduced capital gains tax rates, so long as they follow the rules. If you own property for a certain minimum period of time before selling it, you can pay taxes at a reduced rate on the gain. Currently, the highest tax rate for long-term capital gains is 15%. For short-term capital gains—property held one year or less—or for other ordinary income, the highest rate is 35%.

To qualify for long-term capital gains rates, you must hold the property for more than one year. Not exactly one year—*more* than one year. The first day is the day after you acquired the property. The day you sell it is counted as part of the holding period. If you buy on January 1, 2008, then January 2, 2008, is the first day of the holding period. If you sell on January 1, 2009, then that is exactly one year, and you do not get capital gains treatment.

If you inherit property, you are considered to have owned it for more than one year, whether you really did or not.

What is a 1031 (tax free) exchange?

The *1031 exchange* (pronounced ten-thirty-one), also called a *Starker exchange* or a *like-kind exchange*, is a way of selling real estate and not paying any taxes until sometime in the (hopefully) distant future. Many people call it a tax-free exchange, but the more correct expression would be "tax-deferred" exchange.

Thanks to Mr. Starker, who was the first person to win on this issue with the IRS, you can avoid paying taxes at the time you sell property, but only if you follow the IRS rules exactly. There is no room for error. Almost always, you will need to hire a professional to handle these details for you, but the tax savings will more than pay for the professional fees.

First, you sell your property. This is called the *relinquished property*. All the sale proceeds must be kept in escrow by someone called a *qualified intermediary*. Usually, this is a closing attorney or escrow company. You have 45 days from the sale of your relinquished property to identify the new real estate you want to buy, called the *replacement property*. You can pick up to three properties to identify—or some other alternatives not covered here—but you must buy one of those properties within 180 days of the sale of your relinquished property. If you do it exactly right, you will not pay any taxes on the sale of your relinquished property the year you sell it.

The technical details regarding other requirements can get pretty complicated. For more information, you might want to read Publication 544, "Sales and Other Dispositions of Assets," and Form 8824, "Like Kind Exchanges," available at **www.irs.gov**.

If you are going to do more research, or talk to a professional about this tax savings tool, be sure to:

• request a written example using your particular numbers;

• ask about the transaction expenses of doing the 1031 exchange; and,

• ask if you might not be better off foregoing the 1031 exchange in order to get higher depreciation deductions on the newly purchased property.

Finally, a word of caution. Because of the large tax savings due to a 1031 exchange, some people are willing to pay more for a piece of property than it is really worth. That is because they are under tremendous pressure to identify something before their 45 days runs out. Also, the above-market portion of the purchase price might still cost less than the income taxes they would otherwise have to pay. If you are in a bidding war with an experienced investor, do not assume the property must be worth what he or she is willing to pay. It may be worth that price to that investor because of his or her 1031 pressures. That does not mean the same property is worth that much in your hands. If you have reached the top dollar amount you previously decided on, you should drop out of the bidding.

Can a Subchapter S corporation save taxes for me?

Yes, it can. Please read about this subject in Chapter 2 on partners.

What is all the GO Zone hype I'm reading about?

Promoters all over the United States are marketing investment properties in the Hurricane Katrina–ravaged Florida, Alabama, and Mississippi Gulf Coast areas, officially named the *Gulf Opportunity Zone*, but nicknamed the *GO Zone*. Typically, promoters advertise rental houses or condo units that will give you huge tax write-offs because of accelerated depreciation. They imply that a modest down payment on a $150,000 condo will result in $75,000 of your additional income from this year being tax-free!

Here is the truth: If you buy or build property in the designated counties in those states, you can write off 50% of the basis in the year the property is placed in *service*—made available for rental. Very generally speaking, *basis* is that portion of your purchase price that is allocated to improvements—everything except the land.

Similar tax incentives were in place for a few years after 9/11. It seems reasonable for the federal government to use this vehicle again. Even if the GO Zone benefits are no longer available by the time you read this, something similar may be in the marketplace for some other disaster recovery. Unless the law is amended, GO Zone tax incentives for real estate expire on December 31, 2008.

Think carefully before leaping to take advantage of schemes offered by promoters. There are several items buried in the fine print, or covered by the disclaimer: "Check with your tax professional before investing." These include the following.

- The passive activity rules still apply. Even the $25,000

maximum deductions available for married couples cannot be used if the couple does not actively participate in managing the property. If the condo is in Gulf Shores, Alabama, and you are in Minnesota, it is hard to do that. On the other hand, you might fit within the vacation home exception. Make sure you talk to a tax professional about this.

- You have to weigh any possible tax benefits against your cash flow risks. There is currently a lot of building going on because of the tax advantages. Will you be able to rent out your property, or will it sit vacant while you make mortgage payments for principal, interest, and taxes every month? Insurance is outrageously expensive on the coast right now. Real estate taxes in Florida are also very high.

- With the building boom, unskilled labor is pouring in from all parts of the United States, Mexico, and Central and South America. Developers are literally throwing up condos and subdivisions. You have to wonder—what is the quality of these buildings, and how soon will an investor have to start making expensive repairs?

Think carefully before responding to any advertisement or signing up at an investment seminar. For most investors, the GO Zone hype is just that—smoke and mirrors.

Glossary

A

AAA-Tenant. In speech, referred to as "Triple A Tenant," but written as "AAA-Tenant." A commercial tenant with the best possible credit rating and the least likely possibility of default. Owners can secure better selling prices or better financing terms if they have such tenants in their property.

absorption rate. The rate at which vacant space is leased or purchased over a specified period of time. The absorption rate for commercial property is usually expressed in square feet per year; residential property is quoted in units (homes) per year.

active participation. An IRS term relating to passive activity losses that can be deducted only against passive activity income, not against ordinary income. Rental activities are always passive, unless you are a real estate professional.

adjusted sales price. In an appraisal, the adjusted sales price is obtained when the sales price of a comparable property is adjusted for factors that make it different from the property being appraised.

at-risk rules. IRS rules limiting the deductibility of some losses, which are not allowed to exceed the amount the taxpayer has *at risk*, meaning the total of cash contributions and liability on promissory notes. Under certain circumstances, non-recourse loans secured by real property but not by the individual's guarantee or endorsement may still satisfy the at-risk rules.

B

bankruptcy. Common expression used to mean insolvency, being a condition in which one's liabilities exceed his or her assets, or in which current cash flow is not sufficient to meet current debts.

basis. Tax and accounting term referring to the original acquisition cost (plus or minus adjustments made during the period of ownership) of a property. It is used to determine annual depreciation deductions and eventual gain or loss upon the disposition of the property.

building permit. Written permission from the local government to proceed with construction, substantial repair, demolition, or sign erection on real property.

C

capture rate. The sales or leasing rate of a project, which is usually compared to similar projects in the marketplace.

cash flow. The cash available from an investment after receipt of all revenues and after payment of all bills, or the process of creating cash flow.

cash-on-cash. A tool for investment analysis, being a comparison of the cash flows taken from a property over some period, usually a year, as compared to the original cash investment.

co-insurance. A method of dividing financial responsibility for a loss between the owner and the insurance company.

continuous occupancy clause. Clause frequently contained in the lease of a shopping center anchor tenant, requiring it to remain open and in business for the entire term of its lease.

continuous operations clause. Similar to a continuous occupancy clause, but with better drafting. The continuous operations clause in the lease of a shopping center anchor tenant requires the tenant to remain open at a contractually defined level of operations sufficient to generate the traffic flow necessary to attract ample customers for the other shopping center tenants.

D

deed in lieu of foreclosure. An instrument transferring title to real property to a mortgage lender without the necessity of going through the foreclosure process.

discounted cash flow. Also known as *present value analysis*, it is an approach to analysis of an income-producing property by calculating the present value of a future income stream with the use of a discount rate. The two most common methods are the *internal rate of return* method and the *present value* method.

discrimination. The act of making generalized distinctions among groups of people or things without inquiry into the specific characteristics of individuals within the group. Includes illegal discrimination such as that based on race, color, sex, age, disability, religion, or family status (protected classifications), and legal discrimination such as a bias for or against college graduates or non-smokers. *See also* disparate impact.

disparate impact. The unintentional but still illegal effect of barring certain groups of people from access to housing, credit, goods, or services because of their race, color, sex, age, disability, religion, or family status.

E

economic rent. Market rent; the rent to be reasonably anticipated in the marketplace as opposed to the actual rent.

effective rental rate. True rent, after taking into account rent concessions. Usually expressed as a dollar amount per square foot.

eviction. The process of denying possession to a tenant. It may be actual or constructive.

expense stop. In a commercial lease, a provision that annual rent escalations due to increasing building operating expenses will be stopped, or capped, at a certain amount of increase per year or over the lifetime of the lease.

F

Foreign Investment in Real Property Tax Act (FIRPTA). Federal law designed to assist in the collection of income taxes when foreign owners and investors sell real property or shares in entities that own real property.

G

going concern value. The value of a business in operation, taking into account the goodwill and the value of the income, in addition to hard assets such as real estate and equipment.

H

historic preservation credits. Common name given to the IRS concept of rehabilitation tax credits.

I

index. A statistical indicator that measures changes in the economy in general or particular areas, or a reference point against which measurements are taken for purposes of making future adjustments.

L

lease. An oral or written agreement transferring the right to exclusive use and possession of property for some period of time.

M

mailbox rule. Rule in contract law that says if an offer is made in such a manner that it would be reasonable to assume that another person would accept the offer by placing a letter or other piece of writing in the mail, then acceptance is deemed to have occurred when the writing was placed in the mail, instead of when it was received by the person making the offer.

mechanics' and materialmen's liens. Statutory lien granted in some states to specifically described persons who provide goods or services contributing to the improvement of real property under a contract with the owner or the owner's representative, such as a general contractor.

N

net lease. A lease in which the tenant pays rent plus some portion of the maintenance and operating expenses of a property. *See also* triple net lease.

normal wear and tear. The amount of physical deterioration that occurs with normal use of a property as contemplated by the parties.

P

periodic tenancy. A tenant's right to possess and use property for periods defined by the amount of rent paid.

R

Real Estate Investment Trust (REIT). A special corporation that must invest only in real estate and must distribute at least 90% of its net income in the form of dividends. In exchange, it is allowed to escape any income tax liability at the corporate level.

real property trades or business. Business activities involving real estate, such as development, redevelopment, construction, reconstruction, acquisition, conversion, rental, operations, or management and brokerage, in which real estate professionals must take part in order to make their losses from passive activities deductible.

renewal probability. The average percentage of tenants in a building who are expected to renew at market rental rates at the expiration of their current leases.

rent control. Laws that regulate the rent that can be charged for space.

S

Section 8 housing. Low- and moderate-income housing subsidized by the federal Department of Housing and Urban Development. There are two primary methods of subsidy, *tenant-based* and *project-based*.

T

tenant improvement (TI) allowance. A negotiated sum the landlord is willing to spend to customize space for the needs of a particular tenant.

tenant-in-common properties (TICs). Investment vehicles that allow persons to buy fractional shares of real estate interests directly, rather than through shares of stock, bond certificates, or other intermediate ownership mechanisms.

triple net lease. A lease in which the tenant pays all expenses associated with the property—maintenance, repairs, insurance, and real estate taxes.

trust. The practice of one party, commonly known as a *trustee*, holding legal title to real property or other assets for the benefit of someone else, called a *beneficiary*.

Appendix A SLANG— TALK THE TALK

It does not matter how much you know about a topic; if you do not use the right "insider language," you will be dismissed as a spectator—someone who knows all the rules but has never really played the sport. Here are some fun expressions you will not find in glossaries at the back of typical real estate investment books.

alligator property. A bad deal that is eating up your money.

annual bumps. Rent increases.

BANANA. Build absolutely nothing anywhere near anyone.

big box. A large rectangular building used by major discount retailers like Wal-Mart, Target, and Kmart.

bird dog. Someone who sends you leads.

boomerangers. Baby boomers' children who come back home to live as adults.

bootstrap financing. Creative financing without a formal lender.

bottom-fishing. Shopping for properties at disgracefully low prices.

bricks and mortar. Having a physical presence, instead of being solely Internet-based.

bricks, clicks, and flips. Having stores, websites, and catalogs.

bullet loan. A loan that will be due in full in a few years.

burned-out tax shelter. Real estate that does not have anymore tax benefits.

CBD. Commercial business district; downtown.

condo cowboys. Condo developers who do not know what they are doing.

corner of Main and Main. The middle of downtown.

c-store. A convenience store.

dark store. A large retail store that is still paying rent but closed the doors at that location.

DINK. Dual income, no kids.

doc-in-a-box. Retail medical offices for minor emergencies.

dog. Crummy property with bad problems, like toxic waste or steep ravines.

dry mortgage. A mortgage loan with no personal liability for the borrower.

dummy. A straw man; someone who fronts for another, secret, buyer.

echo boomers. Children of baby boomers.

empty nesters. Baby boomers whose children have grown up and moved out.

equity stripping. (1) Buying foreclosures at deep discounts; or, (2) hiding assets.

fleas. The things that are bad about *dog* properties.

garage mahal. Pretentious garage architecture.

gatekeeper. The person who keeps you from getting to the decision-maker.

gazump. Increasing the sales price after someone agrees to buy but before contract signing.

gazunder. Decreasing the offer after someone agrees to sell but before contract signing.

going dark. Large retailer closing its doors but continuing to pay rent.

gold plating. Padding expenses or financials.

greater fool theory. Even if you pay too much, someone else will pay more.

gross up. Artificially increasing building expenses to a calculated level.

home cooking. Out-of-town lawyers and parties getting the shaft from locals.

house fluffer. Decorator who makes a house look pretty so it will sell more quickly.

house poor. Having a big house, but no cash.

ironclad agreement. No such thing. Any agreement can be successfully broken.

LULUs. Locally unwanted land uses.

McMansion. Pretentious house that looks like all the other pretentious houses.

NFL city. City with an NFL franchise; supposedly has good demographics.

NIMBY. Not in my backyard.

open the kimono. Reveal all financial information to a supposed buyer.

paint-to-paint. What you own in a condo—the insides of the outer walls.

paper. Mortgage notes.

paper the file. Generate a lot of analyses, spreadsheets, charts, and photos for a loan application.

pipeline. What is coming along at the moment in the way of prospects, apartments, condos, etc.

pipeline risk. Lender worry that interest rates will increase after a firm loan commitment.

Popeye property. Nothing glamorous, just a good, solid investment that seems to say, "I yam what I yam."

rack rate. Quoted rent rate, ignoring discounts that might be available.

sandwich lease. A sublease.

scrape. A property suitable only for bulldozing and redevelopment.

seed money. Start-up cash before obtaining any loans.

see-through building. New building with no tenants.

skin in the game. Investor/developer with some cash at risk; not 100% financing.

starter castle. Pretentious home built with really cheap components and methods.

sweat equity. Increase in value due to hard work.

tax ferrets. People who rat out tax cheats.

tornado bait. Mobile home.

underwater. Property with more debt than the property is worth.

upper bracket. Where someone is if he or she is making lots of money.

vanilla building. A plain building that could have any brand of tenant.

vulture capitalist. Someone waiting for a crash so he or she can buy properties very cheaply.

Appendix B CONSUMER PROTECTION LAWS

■ What protection does the Servicemembers Civil Relief Act provide?

■ What is the Truth in Lending Act?

■ What are the TILA disclosures?

■ If I sell some properties and advertise "seller financing available," "no money down," or something similar, will I have to include additional information in my ads?

■ If I require credit checks for potential tenants or for buyers if I will hold some or all of the financing, do any federal laws apply to me?

■ When collecting past due rent from tenants or mortgage payments from buyers, do I have to comply with the Fair Debt Collection Practices Act?

■ If I am a landlord, will I have to learn all the Fair Housing laws?

■ If the federal or state Fair Housing laws apply to me, who is protected from discrimination and who can I legally discriminate against?

■ Do I need to worry about auditors checking to see if I have complied with the Fair Housing laws?

■ Should I concentrate on investments in commercial properties so I do not have to comply with the Fair Housing laws when deciding whether to accept a tenant?

■ What is the Americans With Disabilities Act?

■ If my property is not already handicap-accessible, will I have to make expensive modifications so I am not in violation of the Americans With Disabilities Act?

■ Who is responsible for making premises accessible under the Americans With Disabilities Act, the landlord or the tenant?

■ What requirements does the Americans With Disabilities Act have for new construction?

■ Are there specific statutes that govern the landlord/tenant relationship?

A great many consumer protection laws exist for your benefit and for the protection of other people you encounter in your role as a real estate investor. The following questions will touch on some of the most important consumer protection laws, and give you guidance regarding resources for more in-depth treatment.

What protection does the Servicemembers Civil Relief Act Provide?

The Servicemembers Civil Relief Act requires automatic reduction of home mortgage interest rates to 6% under certain circumstances and a variety of other protections from eviction, lapse of life insurance, garnishments, and lawsuits.

What is the Truth in Lending Act?

The federal law known as *The Consumer Credit Protection Act of 1968* is also called the *Truth in Lending Act*, usually shortened to TILA. It attempts to cure once widespread lending abuse regarding:

- hidden and misleading loan costs; and,
- misleading advertising regarding loans.

Lenders are now required to disclose the true costs of borrowing money so that borrowers can make the best choices. Some states have adopted their own version of TILA called the *Uniform Consumer Credit Code*, which is possibly more stringent than TILA. In the states that have adopted the Uniform Consumer Credit Code, TILA does not apply.

While most lenders comply with Truth in Lending requirements for all their loans, you should be aware that they are not technically required to do so. TILA applies to consumer loans. *Consumers* are defined as people who borrow money primarily for personal, family, or household purposes. Your real estate investments do not fall within that definition. As a result, you should make it a habit to always ask potential lenders for a list of all expenses associated with applying for, evaluating, and closing on a loan with their company. It is not a good idea to rely on them to disclose those costs to you in advance.

When you sell your investment properties, if you hold the financing or engage in some sort of lease/purchase options, you might have to comply with TILA. The federal law applies to everyone who "regularly extends" consumer credit. A footnote to one of the regulations (12 C.F.R. §226.2(a)(17)(i), FN3) says that the word "regularly" applies to anyone who finances more than five home mortgages in a year. The exception is for unusually high interest rate mortgages (as defined in the regulations), in which case even one seller-financed mortgage can bring you within the requirements of TILA.

What are the TILA disclosures?

The four disclosures that must appear in a prominent place are: (1) the amount financed; (2) the finance charge; (3) the annual percentage rate; and, (4) the total of all payments over time. This information should appear in something called the *Regulation Z Box*.

Annual Percentage Rate	Finance Charge	Amount Financed	Total of Payments
The cost of your credit at a yearly rate	The dollar amount the credit will cost you	The amount of credit provided to you or on your behalf	The amount you will have paid after you have made all payments as scheduled
A%	$B	$C	$D

A: The annual cost of the loan as a percentage. Usually higher than the quoted interest rate because of the additional cost of prepaid interest and other finance charges.

B: If all payments are made on time, and the loan is paid in full over its expected term, "B" is the total of all interest, prepaid interest, and mortgage insurance payments over the life of the loan.

C: The loan you applied for, less prepaid interest and other up-front frinance charges such as commitment fees, origination fees, or mortgage insurance premiums paid up front.

D: The toal of all payments (principle, interest, and mortgage insurance) if the loan is paid in full over the entire term.

If I sell some properties and advertise "seller financing available," "no money down," or something similar, will I have to include additional information in my ads?

To answer this question, you have to know if the Federal Truth in Lending laws or your own state consumer credit code apply to you. For guidance, refer back to the question, "What is the Truth in Lending law?"

If these laws apply, then any advertising that contains any *one* of the following "trigger terms" will also have to contain additional information. The trigger terms are:

- amount of down payment (example: "no money down");
- amount of any installment payment (example: "$500 a month

buys this house");
- dollar amount of any finance charge; and,
- the number of installments or the period of repayment (example: "own this home in ten short years").

Using one of the trigger terms will force you to include *all* of the following information in your same ad:

1. the down payment, if any;
2. the terms of repayment; and,
3. the rate of finance charge, expressed as an annual percentage rate.

If I require credit checks for potential tenants or for buyers if I will hold some or all of the financing, do any federal laws apply to me?

The primary law you should be concerned with is the *Fair Credit Reporting Act*. As a landlord or potential mortgage lender, you will also have certain legal responsibilities. In a nutshell, if you turn someone down because of information you obtained from his or her credit report, you must supply him or her with an *adverse action notice*. It must give notice of the adverse action, which would be something like, "Your rental application is rejected." It must also identify the particular credit reporting agency that supplied the information you relied on, and set out the consumer's rights under the Fair Credit Reporting Act.

The Federal Trade Commission (FTC) has guidance, in the form of a pamphlet entitled *Using Consumer Reports: What Landlords Need to Know*. You can obtain a copy by going to the FTC website at **www.ftc.gov**. At the top of the page, select "consumer protection," then "Business Information." Then, under the heading "Business Catagories," select "Credit," and then "Consumer Reports." Finally, click on the article titled "Using Consumer Reports: What Landlords Need to Know." Or you can write to:

The FTC Consumer Response Center
Room 130
600 Pennsylvania Avenue NW
Washington, DC 20580

When collecting past due rent from tenants or mortgage payments from buyers, do I have to comply with the Fair Debt Collection Practices Act?

The federal law known as the *Fair Debt Collection Practices Act* applies to individuals and companies who collect debts for other people. In other words, if you or your employees are attempting to collect money from your own tenants or borrowers, then the law does not apply.

This does not mean you can engage in any sort of abusive, threatening, or harassing behavior to collect. Particular states might have their own statutes that apply to you or that specifically address tenant rights. Additionally, people might be able to sue you under general principles of law, such as for intentional infliction of emotional distress, outrage, slander, or invasion of privacy. I find that complying with consumer protection laws, even if they do not specifically apply to me, is usually the safest course.

Tip: To obtain more information about the Fair Debt Collection Practices Act, visit the Federal Trade Commission website at **www.ftc.gov**. At the top of the page, select "Consumer Protection," then "Consumer Information." Under the heading "Consumer Categories," select "Credit & Loans," and then "In Debt?" Finally, click on the article titled "Fair Debt Collection," or you can call 877-FTC-HELP (877-382-4357).

In a nutshell, credit collectors may not:

• harass debtors by using threats of violence, publishing a list of *deadbeats*, using obscene or profane language, making repeated phone calls to annoy you, making phone calls early in the morning or late at night, or calling you at work if you advise them you are not allowed to receive such calls;

• make any false or misleading statements, such as implying they will press criminal charges for the debt, saying or giving the impression they are lawyers if they are not, giving the impression that papers being sent to you are legal forms, using a false name or misrepresenting the amount of the debt; or,

• engage in unfair practices, such as sending correspondence on a publicly viewable postcard, making an early deposit of a post-dated check, or using deception to make you pay for collect phone calls.

If I am a landlord, will I have to learn all the Fair Housing laws?

The federal *Fair Housing* laws are intended to stop housing discrimination and to make sure that everyone has open access to housing choices. It outlaws flagrant discrimination—such as refusing to rent to certain minorities—and subtle discrimination—such as steering potential tenants to housing with a higher percentage of "people like them." As with all other federal consumer protection laws, there are categories that are exempt from the requirements; however, you are treading on dangerous ground if you attempt to discriminate because you think you can get away with it. State statutes or general common law might impose similar responsibilities on you.

The Fair Housing law exemptions are sometimes called the "Mom

& Pop exemptions." The federal law does not apply to single-family homes sold or rented by the owner or duplexes and triplexes rented by the owner, but only if the owner does not:

- use the services of a real estate agent for the investment properties;
- use any discriminatory advertising;
- own more than three rental units (the owner can own a quadraplex, but only if he or she lives in one of the units); or,
- sell more than one house in twenty-four months in which he or she was not the most recent resident.

Remember, your state may not allow these exceptions. If your state's Fair Housing laws are more restrictive than the federal ones, then the state laws will apply. To find out the situation in your particular state, call a local housing assistance office, HUD office, or your attorney general or state attorney's office for guidance. You can also search the Internet using the name of your state and the phrase "fair housing law."

If the federal or state Fair Housing laws apply to me, who is protected from discrimination and who can I legally discriminate against?

Fair Housing laws start with the premise that people who fit certain descriptions have historically suffered from unfair housing discrimination. These categories are called *protected classifications*. You are not allowed to discriminate against people who fit into any of the following categories. Under federal law, they are:

- race and color
- national origin
- religion
- gender

- families with children under 18 or pregnant women
- disability

Some state laws also forbid housing discrimination based on:

- military status
- sexual orientation
- source of income
- affiliation (usually mixed-race marriages or relationships)

You can place reasonable limits on the number of occupants of the housing, but the limits must apply to all types of occupants. In most states, you can refuse housing to persons convicted of a crime so long as your standards are consistent. You cannot discriminate against Hispanics convicted of any crime and white persons only if they have been convicted of a felony, for example. You can refuse to rent to someone with poor credit, no credit, to students, or to non-students.

You may discriminate against younger persons if the housing is targeted toward older persons. The senior housing exemption has the following specific requirements.

- HUD has determined that the dwelling is specifically designed for and occupied by elderly persons under a federal, state, or local government program.
- It is occupied solely by persons who are 62 or older.
- It houses at least one person who is 55 or older in at least 80% of the occupied units, and adheres to a policy that demonstrates intent to house persons who are 55 or older.

Do I need to worry about auditors checking to see if I have complied with the Fair Housing laws?

Auditors are the least of your worries. In most instances, you will be below the radar of any government regulators looking for violations. On the other hand, private individuals may legally pretend to seek housing, catch you in a violation, and sue you for money damages and legal fees. The U.S. Supreme Court has ruled that even if such persons never had any intention of buying or renting anything at all and simply set you up, they can still maintain a lawsuit. There are many individuals and groups in the country who do this as a career. Your insurance company may be able to provide valuable guidance to assist you in avoiding such problems.

Should I concentrate on investments in commercial properties so I do not have to comply with the Fair Housing laws when deciding whether to accept a tenant?

By definition, the fair housing laws apply only to housing. You may run afoul of other state and federal laws if you attempt to discriminate against certain tenants based on their status in one of the protected classifications. Those laws are beyond the scope of this book.

What is the Americans With Disabilities Act?

The *Americans With Disabilities Act* (ADA) is a federal law that grants civil rights protections to individuals with disabilities. It guarantees equal opportunity for individuals with disabilities in public accommodations, employment, transportation, state and local government services, and telecommunications.

As related to real estate, the ADA is most relevant in its provisions regarding public accommodation. Responsibility for compliance is placed on both landlords and tenants, as well as other property owners. Many commercial leases allocate the burden of ADA compliance so that the tenant must pay for any alterations or improvements necessary to bring a property into compliance.

Places of public accommodation include a wide range of entities, such as restaurants, hotels, theaters, doctors' offices, pharmacies, retail stores, museums, libraries, parks, private schools, and day care centers. Private clubs and religious organizations are exempt.

If my property is not already handicap-accessible, will I have to make expensive modifications so I am not in violation of the Americans With Disabilities Act?

Two different laws might apply to you in regard to persons with disabilities. The federal Fair Housing Law says you cannot discriminate against persons with disabilities, and you must make something called *reasonable accommodations* if requested. There are no specific rules regarding what is a reasonable accommodation, except that the cost of the accommodation is one factor that plays into how reasonable it is. For example, someone with a prosthetic leg might request that you place a reserved sign at the parking place in front of his or her unit even though you do not have reserved parking. This would be a reasonable accommodation. A request to install an elevator in a two-story house would be unreasonable.

ADA accesibility guidelines are as follows.

- *Accessibility for existing properties*—Must take steps to remove barriers if it can be done easily and without much expense. The evaluation of the expense depends on the size and financial strength of the entity.

- *Accessibility requirements when a property undergoes alteration or renovation*—For example, if during renovations a doorway is being relocated, the new doorway must be wide enough to meet the new construction standard for accessibility. When alterations are made to a primary function area, such as the lobby of a bank or the dining area of a cafeteria, an accessible path of travel to the altered area must also be provided. The bathrooms, telephones, and drinking fountains serving that area must also be made accessible. These additional accessibility alterations are only required to the extent that the added accessibility costs do not exceed 20% of the cost of the original alteration.

- *Accessibility in new construction*—The ADA requires that all new construction of places of public accommodation, as well as of commercial facilities, such as office buildings, be accessible. Elevators are generally not required in facilities under three stories or with fewer than 3,000 square feet per floor, unless the building is a shopping center or mall; the professional office of a health care provider; a terminal, depot, or other public transit station; or an airport passenger terminal.

- *Litigation*—Private individuals may bring lawsuits to obtain injunctive relief to force compliance with the ADA and recover their attorney's fees for the litigation, but may not obtain money damages. Citizens may also file complaints with the U.S. attorney general, who is authorized to bring lawsuits in cases of general public importance or where a pattern of discrimination is alleged. The suit can ask for money damages and civil penalties.

You can find more information on the official ADA website at: **www.usdoj.gov/crt/ada.**

Who is responsible for making premises accessible under the Americans With Disabilities Act, the landlord or the tenant?

Both the landlord and the tenant are equally responsible under the federal law. The lease can designate who will be responsible for any modifications, but that controls only the relationship between the landlord and the tenant. They are also both still liable in the case of any third parties.

What requirements does the Americans With Disabilities Act have for new construction?

The ADA requires that all new construction of places of public accommodation, as well as of commercial facilities, such as office buildings, be accessible. Elevators are generally not required in facilities under three stories or with fewer than 3,000 square feet per floor, unless the building is a shopping center or mall; the professional office of a health care provider; a terminal, depot, or other public transit station; or, an airport passenger terminal. ADA requirements are usually written into local building codes. Check with the building code or inspections departments of your city or county government offices. They can provide you with additional assistance and resources.

Are there specific statutes that govern the landlord/ tenant relationship?

All states have laws that spell out landlord and tenant rights and responsibilities in the area of housing. Some also have laws regarding business tenants. Provisions can cover things like security deposits, minimum standards for heat, water, and security, late fees, notice requirements before entry on premises, and eviction procedures. There is no federal landlord/tenant law, except as fair housing and other such laws might apply to the relationship.

Appendix C RUN THE NUMBERS

- Do I need to learn any accounting in order to successfully invest in real estate?
- What accounting concepts do I need to know?
- Should I buy any specialized tax software?
- I am planning to buy a house, rehab it, and then sell. How can I calculate my profit?
- How do I calculate my after-tax profit from a property sale?
- What is a pro forma?
- What is an APOD?
- Where can I get an APOD form?
- How can I estimate property value using the NOI?
- Can you give an example of cap rate changes affecting property values?
- Can you give an example of NOI changes affecting property values?

Do I need to learn any accounting in order to successfully invest in real estate?

No, you do not need to learn accounting per se, but you need some simple arithmetic skills—about as much as what you use to balance your checkbook.

This is not to say you should ignore accounting. Accounting serves two purposes. Most people pay attention to only one purpose—historical information. Financial reports will tell you how well you did last month, last year, or five years ago. Financial reports will also assist in the preparation of your tax returns. More importantly, the reports should be used to make decisions for the future—the second purpose. The following are possible questions that financial reports can help you answer.

1. If my three-bedroom, two-bathroom apartment units are always full, should I raise the rent on that size apartment but not the other sizes?

2. After looking at all my maintenance expenses for the past several years, would it be cheaper to hire a part-time or full-time maintenance person?

3. How much do I spend renting specialized tools for rehab projects? Would it be cheaper to buy the tools?

4. How much am I spending on real estate commissions, what is the average time my properties are on the market, and would I be better off cutting my selling price and listing on MLS with a discount broker instead of hiring a real estate agent?

5. If I took one apartment out of the rental pool and converted it

to a laundry room or rentable storage lockers, how would that affect my bottom line?

6. My leases have a ten-day grace period before there is a late charge. Most tenants pay on the ninth or tenth day of the month. Should I shorten the grace period to five days?

7. What am I spending each year on plumbing repairs? Why? Do I need to overhaul the whole plumbing system, better insulate the pipes, revise my lease so I can charge certain things back to tenants, or do a better job of charging tenants for repairs made necessary by their actions?

What accounting concepts do I need to know?

There are a very few simple accounting principles that will help you.

Cash basis accounting means you post income when you receive it, and you post bills when you pay them. If a tenant pays the rent on January 1, it is January income. If the tenant is late and pays on February 1, along with the February rent, then you have no income in January and twice as much as normal in February. A bill received in March but paid in April will be an April expense. This method has the benefit of being easy, but the drawback of not being very accurate.

Accrual basis accounting means you post income when you have earned it, and you post expenses when you receive the bill. If you were doing this manually, with paper and pencil, it would require several steps to handle each transaction. Most software will take care of posting things to the right period if you just tell the software during setup that you want accrual basis accounting. The system has the benefit of allowing you to match income against expenses in the right periods and to do better planning for the future.

If you use accrual basis accounting, then bad debts—such as uncollectible rent—should always be posted as an expense. You enter the income as if you received the rent, and then you enter the same amount as a bad debt expense. The net result is $0, so there is no profit and no tax. But, you can keep track of how large your bad debts are each year in case you need to make decisions about doing things differently.

If you use accrual basis accounting, then anything you give away for free—such as first month free rent—should be listed as an expense. You would enter the rent you should have received as income, and then enter the one month's free rent as an expense. This does not affect your profitability or your taxes. It does let you look at your accounting reports to see how much free stuff you are giving away, and if you might want to change your policy. Otherwise, the giveaways just get overlooked because you have no way to track them.

Some things are legitimate business expenses but are not tax deductible—like entertainment expenses. Do not let tax considerations rule how you keep track of expenses. If it is a legitimate business expense, show it in your bookkeeping. Your accountant or tax accounting software can do something called *book-to-tax adjustment* to correct for items that are not fully deductible.

Should I buy any specialized tax software?

If you are going to buy rental properties, invest in one of the property management software packages. QuickBooks by Intuit Software has a good version for beginners, called Quicken Rental Property Manager. I also like something called RentRight. It has the additional benefit of tracking work orders for things like repairs. This lets you know what work remains to be completed, how the actual costs compare to estimates, and which tenants generate the most work orders, and it charges some or all of the repair expenses back to specific tenants.

House flippers should buy a QuickBooks version designed specifically for contractors. It will help you keep track of all acquisition and construction expenses accurately. I recommend the Premier Contractor version because it allows you to track change orders, track your job status, and enter yourself as a subcontractor at a $1 an hour billing rate in order to help you keep track of your own time spent on the project.

Most accounting software companies will set up some kind of software with your information for a small fee or refer you to independent companies in your area that do the same thing. This is probably money well spent on your part if you are not comfortable with accounting concepts.

I am planning to buy a house, rehab it, and then sell. How can I calculate my profit?

Here is a worksheet to help you calculate expenses and your profit before taxes. Your project lender or local government may require additional expense estimations besides the ones listed on the table. Be sure to modify this table as needed. You will have to obtain quotes from local people, but at least the worksheet will help you think about all the expenses involved. The first column is for estimated expenses and the next one is for actual expenses. If you copy this form and use it on all your projects, you will be able to prepare much

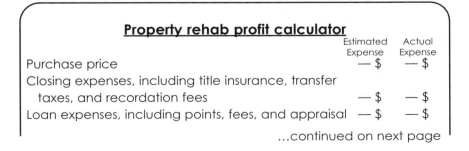

Property rehab profit calculator

	Estimated Expense	Actual Expense
Purchase price	— $	— $
Closing expenses, including title insurance, transfer taxes, and recordation fees	— $	— $
Loan expenses, including points, fees, and appraisal	— $	— $

...continued on next page

Construction permit and inspection fees, if any	— $	— $
Builder's risk insurance	— $	— $
Temporary utilities, port-a-potty	— $	— $
Debris removal, dumpster	— $	— $
Repairs: electrical	— $	— $
Repairs: plumbing	— $	— $
Repairs: HVAC	— $	— $
Repairs: roof	— $	— $
Repairs: windows and doors	— $	— $
Repairs: rough carpentry	— $	— $
Repairs: finish carpentry	— $	— $
Repairs: drywall	— $	— $
Paint & wallcoverings	— $	— $
Carpet & floor coverings	— $	— $
Landscaping	— $	— $
Other:	— $	— $
Construction period interest payments, loan disbursement fees, real estate taxes	— $	— $
Anticipated sales price	+ $	+ $
Marketing & advertising	— $	— $
Sales commissions & fees	— $	— $
Seller's closing expenses	— $	— $
Profit before taxes		

more accurate estimates over time.

How do I calculate my after-tax profit from a property sale?

To calculate your after-tax profit, you must know your marginal tax rate for state and federal income taxes. The rates are based on your taxable income (TI), which is the amount remaining after adjustments and deductions.

2006 Tax Year: Single Taxpayers

If TI is over:	But not over:	The tax is:
$0	$7,550	10% of the amount over $0
$7,550	$30,650	$755 plus 15% of the amount over $7,550
$30,650	$74,200	$4,220.00 plus 25% of the amount over $30,650
$74,200	$154,800	$15,107.50 plus 28% of the amount over $74,200
$154,800	$336,550	$37,675.50 plus 33% of the amount over $154,800
$336,550	no limit	$97,653.00 plus 35% of the amount over $336,550

2006 Tax Year: Married Filing Joint Returns

If TI is over:	But not over:	The tax is:
$0	$15,100	10% of the amount over $0
$15,100	$61,300	$1,510 plus 15% of the amount over $15,100
$61,300	$123,700	$8,440 plus 25% of the amount over $61,300
$123,700	$188,450	$24,040 plus 28% of the amount over $123,700
$188,450	$336,550	$42,170 plus 33% of the amount over $188,450
$336,550	no limit	$91,043 plus 35% of the amount over $336,550

Unless you are right on the cusp of a bracket change, you can usually take the percentage amount for the bracket you are in and multiply that percentage by your profit to calculate federal taxes. Do not forget to also subtract state income taxes, if there are any in your state.

What is a pro forma?

A *pro forma* is an estimate of the expenses associated with a project and the anticipated revenues and profits. It is used to evaluate whether you should go forward with the deal or not, and it is given to lenders in support of any loan request you make. The more detailed your pro forma and the more documentation you can supply in support of your numbers, the better your chance of obtaining a loan. Do not allow yourself to be dismissed as naïve, unrealistic, or wildly optimistic. I like to supply lenders with three pro formas—most likely case, worst case, and best case. That way, they know I have dreamed about the best, prepared for the worst, and settled on something that seems realistic. It gives me more credibility.

For a house flip, a pro forma consists of the Property Rehab Profit Calculator form provided earlier in this appendix. It should include all additional line items that might be applicable to your project. An income-producing property pro forma would include the following forms, which are explained in the following pages.

1. APOD;
2. cash flow; and
3. NOI/Cap Rate Calculator (which also appears later in this appenix).

What is an APOD?

APOD stands for *Annual Property Operating Data*. If you are investing in income-producing property, the APOD form helps you account for all income and expenses associated with the property. It then provides the basis for estimating the property value, using the NOI/Cap Rate Calculator. All commercial real estate brokers and all lenders use some version of the APOD form.

> **Tip:** One thing that routinely troubles new investors is how to handle mortgage payments when calculating property expenses. For income tax purposes, mortgage interest payments are deductible expenses. Mortgage principal payments are not deductible.

For APOD purposes, mortgage payments are irrelevant and not included at all. Remember, the "O" in APOD is for "Operating." Mortgage payments are not a cost of *operating* a property; they are, rather, a cost of *acquiring* property. You might have a large mortgage loan, a small one, or none at all. None of these scenarios has anything to do with how well the property performs. Loan payments affect your *personal* cash flow—the money available to buy other things—but not property operating revenues and expenses.

Where can I get an APOD form?

I have reprinted a very simple version of an APOD, with explanations of the various entries. Remember that the "A" in APOD stands for "annual." Enter total amounts for the entire year, not monthly figures.

```
┌─────────────────────────────────────────────────────────────┐
│                     Simplified APOD                          │
│            (all numbers calculated on annual basis)          │
│  Total potential rental income (PRI)                  + $    │
│  Vacancy and credit losses                            – $    │
│  Effective rental income                              = $    │
│  Other income (late fees, laundry room, forfeited security   │
│     deposits)                                         + $    │
│  Gross operating income (effective rental income plus        │
│     other income)                                     = $    │
│  Real estate taxes                                    – $    │
│  Personal property taxes (e.g, furniture in furnished        │
│     apartments)                                       – $    │
│  Insurance                                            – $    │
│  Off-site management (management company.                    │
│  If you self-manage, include a figure for yourself of 8%     │
│  of Gross Operating Income)                           – $    │
│  Payroll (gross pay + taxes, benefits, & workers compensation)– $ │
│  Repairs and maintenance (does not include capital           │
│     expenditures like roof replacement, parking lot repaving,│
│     or large scale rehab)                             – $    │
│  Utilities                                            – $    │
│  Accounting and legal (includes collection expenses)  – $    │
│  Licenses, permits, and rental taxes                  – $    │
│  Advertising                                          – $    │
│  Supplies                                             – $    │
│  Misc. contract services (lawn care, pool maintenance) – $   │
│  Total Operating Expenses                             = $    │
│  Net Operating Income (Gross Operating Income minus          │
│     Total Operating Expenses) Usually shortened to NOI = $   │
└─────────────────────────────────────────────────────────────┘
```

How can I estimate property value using the NOI?

Most income-producing property is evaluated using the NOI and an appropriate *cap rate*. Conceptually, the *cap rate* is the annual interest rate you would like to earn on that particular investment. Before you would be willing to buy an apartment complex in a rundown part of town, you might want to make sure you can earn at least a 15% annual return on the purchase price. For a brand-new apartment complex three blocks from a college campus, you might be willing to earn as little as 5% on your purchase price because it is such a safe investment. Cap rates are a little like the stock market in that they are a function of what buyers will pay, what sellers will take, and what lenders will finance. They can move over a wide range in just a few short years.

The NOI and cap rate evaluation always assume you pay cash for the property, even if you obtain 80% or 100% financing.

This is the arithmetic behind the calculation:

1. Before I will buy this property, it must earn 15% of its purchase price every year.
2. This property earns—has an NOI—of $75,000 per year.
3. 15% of what number gives you $75,000?
4. Using algebra, you find the number by dividing $75,000 by 0.15, which gives you $500,000.
5. If an investment costs $500,000 and earns $75,000 per year, then it earns 15%
6. You can spend no more than $500,000 for this property if you require a cap rate of 15% before you will invest.

To estimate value based on the NOI and your personal require-ments regarding a cap rate, you always divide NOI by the cap rate (expressed as a decimal—7% is 0.07 and 15% is 0.15) to arrive at the number.

In the example above, the apartment complex might actually be worth more than $500,000. Willing buyers in the marketplace might be willing to pay $750,000 for it, which would be the true value. In that case, the true market cap rate on those types of properties would be 10%. If you had a similar property and wanted to estimate its value, you would use a cap rate of 10% because you know investors are willing to pay purchase prices based on a 10% cap rate.

Can you give an example of cap rate changes affecting property values?

My husband develops first-class self-storage facilities with climate-controlled storage, individual door alarms, and all the bells and whis-tles necessary for high-end properties. Within the last six or seven years, cap rates in this industry for similar properties have moved from 11% down to 6.5% and are now creeping back up again. The chart below shows what simple cap rate changes will do to value for the same property, earning the same rental rates and incurring the same expenses with no new competition in the area. Let us assume an NOI of $100,000 per year.

How Cap Rates Affect Value on an NOI of $100,000

Cap Rate	Value
11%	$909,090
10%	$1,000,000
9%	$1,111,111
8%	$1,250,000
7%	$1,428,571
6.5%	$1,538,461

If this property were sold when cap rates were lowest, rather than when they were highest, the owner would make an extra $629,371.

Can you give an example of NOI changes affecting property values?

The magic of always thinking about NOI and cap rates is that it causes you to be very sensitive to small increases in revenues and small decreases in expenses. That is because these relatively minor changes can have a dramatic effect upon the value of the property, even if they do not seem to significantly affect the amount of cash you put in your pocket at the end of each month.

For example, let us assume you have a quadraplex. The monthly rent for each unit is $800 and the NOI for the property is $31,000. You decide that if you spend $1,000 on landscaping, $2,000 on new appliances, and build some balconies and patios at a cost of $1,500, you could raise the rents by $50 per month. You might not think it is worth the trouble to spend $3,800 just to earn an extra $2,400 per year. But, none of those expenditures are operating expenses—they are capital expenses to increase the value of the property, which means they do not affect the NOI. The increase in rents does affect the NOI, and raises it by $2,400 from the prior $31,000 to $33,400. The chart below shows what happens to value:

How Increasing Rents Adds to Value	
Former NOI	$31,000
Current cap rates	9%
Value	$344,444
New NOI	$33,400
Current cap rates	9%
New value	$371,111
Increase in value	$26,667

As you can see, spending $3,800 increases the value by over $26,000. Small changes can have dramatic effects.

Index

About the

Denise L. Evans received her law degree from the University of Alabama Law School, with a concentration in real estate, tax, and finance. While a law student, she served on the Board of Editors for the Journal of the Legal Profession, published two scholarly articles, was Director of the Legal Research Department, and clerked with a law firm that had a large real estate practice. She graduated at the top of her class, earning the prestigious Henderson M. Somerville Prize. Afterwards, she spent several year related to real estate. At rtment of eight litig or lawyers througho

Today, s ted busi-nesses, i al million dollars. practice. She has d passing on her lementing them he

Never c s, a candi-date for) designa-tion. M hapter of CREW te for the Alabam Alabama. She or town, and serves

She res lf a million honeyb ssful peace on Lak